TRACKS

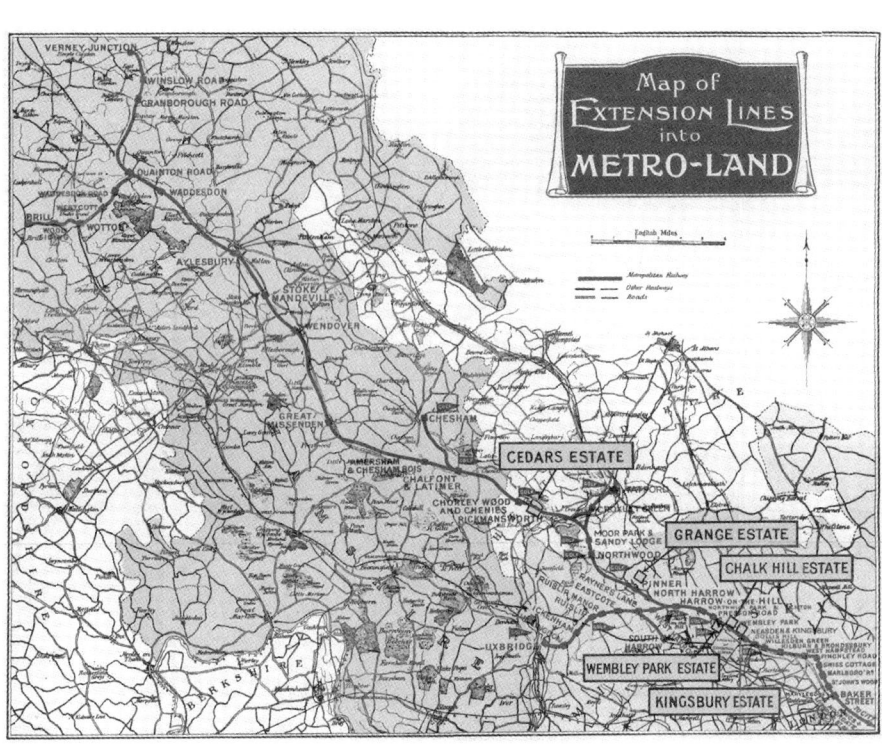

TRACKS

A Journey Through Metro-land

KEVIN J LAST

To my wife, whose life was largely destroyed by Covid-19.

Published in 2026 by Unicorn an imprint of Unicorn Publishing Group
Charleston Studio
Meadow Business Centre
Lewes BN8 5RW
www.unicornpublishing.org

Text © Kevin J. Last

Kevin J. Last has asserted his moral right under the Copyright, Designs and Patents Act 1988 to be identified as the author of this work.

All rights reserved. No part of the contents of this book may be reproduced, stored in or introduced into a retrieval system, or transmitted, in any form or by any means (electronic, mechanical, photocopying, recording or otherwise), without the prior written permission of the copyright holder and the above publisher of this book.

Every effort has been made to trace copyright holders and to obtain their permission for the use of copyrighted material. The publisher apologises for any errors or omissions and would be grateful to be notified of any corrections that should be incorporated in future reprints or editions of this book.

ISBN 978-1-917458-32-0
10 9 8 7 6 5 4 3 2 1

Designed by Mach 3 Solutions
Printed by Fine Tone Ltd in Latvia

CONTENTS

Introduction	1
Small Beginnings	13
A Brief History of the Metropolitan Line	40
Electrification	49
Sir Edward Watkin	55
The Rise of Metro-land	62
Onwards and Outwards	74
The Uxbridge Branch	88
The Ruislip Connection	94
The Chess Valley and Beyond	98
Points West	111
In Search of Cymbeline	118
More Recently	135
Conclusions	137
Acknowledgements	140
Bibliography and Filmography	141
Index	143

N.B. Quotations from books quote the page number then the year of publication, while web pages simply quote the year of access or publication if known.

Early Electric! Sit you down and see,
'Mid this fine woodwork and a smell of dinner,
A stained-glass windmill and a pot of tea,
And sepia views of leafy lanes in PINNER, –
Then visualize, far down the shining lines,
Your parents' homestead set in murmuring pines.

From *The Metropolitan Railway* by John Betjeman

INTRODUCTION

This book starts with one irony and ends with another. When most of the main railway routes in this country were being built in the 19th century, the Victorian visionaries who constructed them did so with a beguiling sense of purpose and determination. When the majority of the main lines had been completed by the early 20th century, the politicians who were overall responsible for their ongoing future had no idea how to manage them, creating one problem after another through a lack of management skills and a resultant dither and delay. The upshot was that a system that we gave the world and that should have been a matter of great pride for the nation turned into an inadequate ragbag of ownership; first private, then public, then private and now possibly nationalised again. Consequently, European railways, which admittedly had the advantage of more space, ploughed well ahead of this country, leaving us in an unholy mess, made worse by Dr Richard Beeching, that has never been sorted out, and a system plagued by inadequacies and strikes set up by militant unions. I have no doubt that some of the lines that Beeching ear-marked for closure were carrying so few passengers that they needed to be cut. However, there was such an outcry when Beeching also wanted to close major hubs like Canterbury, Hereford, Inverness and Salisbury that these were left *in situ*. Not all of the cuts attributed to Beeching were actually carried out by him, since in 1964 the Labour Party closed around 1,400 more stations after Beeching had completed his demolition. There was even a programme of closures before he came on the scene, but he took most of the well-deserved blame: some of these were vital links, especially in the West Country where Brixham, Lyme Regis, Padstow and Ilfracombe all lost their stations. The subsequent mess is therefore easily understandable. Anyone who has ever travelled from Paddington to Penzance knows that it takes just under six hours to travel the 280-mile journey. As Matthew Engel tells us, "it is like *rigor mortis* with scenery", it is so slow.

Engel also tells us, in a brief summary of other country's railways, that

> The only other country that proceeded in anything like the British manner was the United States, where federalism, size and the national culture made government control improbable. Often American railroads were cheap and cheerful rickety lines thrown across the prairies where there were no snotty aristocrats to try to out-greed the railway barons (which would have been some feat), merely the Indians and the buffalo whose role was to be shot at and stay dead. (85, 2009)

A little simplistic and perhaps somewhat misinformed by watching too many Westerns.

> The cheerfulness was a necessity because the distances were so vast and the trains so slow... But the infrastructure rotted, producing a railway that became the reverse of the British one: vital for shifting bulk freight across the continent, but almost wholly useless for passengers [despite the introduction of the Pullman car]. (85, 2009)

But they did become useful for transporting large numbers of troops who were necessarily less concerned about their creature comforts. This applied in the UK as well.

Engel also comments on some of the other European countries to illustrate that we were not entirely alone with our problems.

> Nineteenth-century travellers found that funny foreign railways had their peculiarities. Second class on German railways (according to *The Railway Traveller's Handy Book of Hints, Suggestions and Advice* (1862)) was so comfortable that there was no point in travelling first class except to avoid the universal habit of smoking. Luggage regulations there, not surprisingly, were rigidly enforced.
>
> Dutch trains were "liberally conducted" (which presumably did not mean the use of marijuana was permitted). However, the author did not recommend Belgian second class to ladies because of a shortage of doors: "The seats... have to be clambered over in the most awkward and indelicate fashion".
>
> Having adopted the gauge and in some cases the left-hand rule of the road, none of these countries sought to emulate Britain's let-a-hundred-flowers-bloom approach to building the system. Sweden briefly got itself entangled with John Sadleir, a fraudster-MP... who, as chairman of The Royal Swedish Railway Company, issued himself

with 20,000 extra shares. On discovery in 1856, he poisoned himself on Hampstead Heath. (84/5, 2009)

Why do these rogues always end up in the UK?

I mention the above so that you can understand some of the inherent difficulties of running a railway, not just with the track but also with the rolling stock. So while the British may believe they were singled out for some of the worst treatment at the hands of the railway companies, other countries found that not everything was plain sailing. I particularly enjoyed a recent account of a grossly busy and very stuffy train in the UK where the staff, aware of the problem, encouraged the passengers to get out at an interim station en route for a breather, which they did to relieve the discomforts of a warm day, only for the service to suddenly set off again without them. At least it alleviated the overcrowding.

However, I doubt that any other European country would have allowed the wholesale destruction of so many important routes. The result of this was to leave somewhat isolated certain communities that had grown up around the development of the railways, the very opposite of what the railways were supposed to achieve. It beggars belief how Beeching was permitted to undertake this without any apparent opposition. YouTube has recently included some short films about abandoned stations in various parts of the country; it is quite fascinating to watch how these old, once-functional buildings gradually get drawn back into the landscape, with some being put to good use in the modern age. What is extraordinary is that, even within one county, there are just so many of them. This, if nothing else, illustrates the scale of Beeching's desecration, a state that only now do we fully seem to be waking up to. It left some areas of the country woefully short of railway transport at a time of increased population growth, and forced more traffic onto our already overcrowded roads.

Whenever I visit a new area, I always try to seek out lost stations, monuments to the past. Some of course have been completely destroyed and replaced by industrial estates, but road names often provide a clue that there was once a station there. Sadly, we continue to lack anyone with the vision to manage the overall network long term, someone who can see the requirements for the future. As a result, any improvements have largely come from local pressure groups or volunteers anxious to restore the importance of their local area in this way.

Despite this, the railways have always held a strange allure for the public. Of all the machines invented or progressed in the 19th century, the railway engine stands alone. Unlike the huge factories, mills and coal mines where men, women and children worked under sometimes appalling conditions, the iron horse has a special place in the hearts of the British (remember Dale Robertson in the TV series *Tales of Wells Fargo*?), despite being an extremely labour-intensive beast and belching out semi-toxic fumes that could be lethal in an enclosed space like a tunnel or, worse still, underground.

The rails themselves offer a continuous metal route to wherever we want to go, usually completely unfettered by other people and other traffic, a bonus when compared with our overcrowded roads. Even standing on a suburban station waiting for a train and glancing down the line for the first sign that our train is approaching, once from steam and later from the headlight of an electric train, conjures up a certain romance of anticipation. The country halt, often disturbed only by birdsong, is even better, the rails reflecting the sun and curving away into the distance towards an unknown destination. The railway companies took advantage of this romance, designing posters to encourage the public to transport them to an idyllic seaside or countryside destination, unthreatened by anything nasty. And the public fell for it. Even now, many railway adverts, like the current one celebrating 200 years of the railways, hark back to this Never Never Land that promised a sunlit world, even if it was often unable to deliver it.

This is, of course, no different from what politicians of different stripes have been doing for hundreds of years, promising us "sunlit uplands" where all our troubles will dissipate. But it was always jam tomorrow, with the onus on us complying in certain ways to achieve the desired result. Of course, those "sunlit uplands" always remain tantalisingly out of reach, and these days the politicos don't even promise anything better; more likely a harsher period symbolised by cuts and loss of benefits, with no guarantee of improvement. But the railways still have an allure, inefficiently run as they may be, and concentrating on one route, the Metropolitan Line, is what this book is all about. The Met was one of only two underground lines that stretched out into the country from a London base, the other being the Central Line heading into Essex.

Of course, in this ultra-modern age, where the motive power has changed to diesel and then electric, many steam locomotives appear beautifully designed and painted. In those changes, the people who ran the railways forgot about what made trains a great innovation, removing the named expresses in favour of a bland response where one train looks very much like another, with only the paint job to distinguish it. Pride in the railways, once foremost, has now disappeared.

Our love affair with steam meant we were among the last to dispose of steam trains from the main routes, only to find them re-emerging in the form of more than a hundred heritage railways, for which the nation has a quite extraordinary affection. We also still retain an unusual number of diesel engines, long after Europe has largely ditched them in favour of the much cleaner electric traction.

I do not believe in electric cars in their present form – one look at a two-hour traffic jam on the A303 on a cold December day should explain that – but I do believe in electric trains. Prescribed routes, computerised signalling and consequent spacing means that these can work excellently. The same approach was adopted by Sir Edward Watkin in his vision for the Metropolitan Line running from London to the north-west suburbs, and despite early difficulties, it was a massive success. But this book is concerned not just with the line but the land surrounding it. The Met managed a dual achievement in both creating a useful route and cannily advertising its surrounds as the best place to live. I intend to describe how it affected both my childhood and the lives of countless commuters in the twentieth century.

I remember lying on a bench atop the cricket field in my final few days at school wondering what life would bring. I was 18 and it seemed a pivotal moment, when exams were over and school no longer held any meaningful place in my life. The stranglehold that it had exercised had been replaced by an uncertain future. I recall looking up at the clouds for inspiration, but they told me nothing. I did not realise then that life is only partly controlled by human intervention; we are in fact governed by other much vaguer and less malleable things like opportunity, health and good luck. And whereas, at that moment, I thought that life had not properly begun, in reality it had already been in operation for probably more than a fifth of my time on this planet.

What was also not fully appreciated at 18 was my relationship with Metro-land. At the time I did not see it as anything other than part of the natural order of things, but looking back, I can see that it occupied quite a significant place in my life, because it was involved, even slightly, in so many of my days. I could always hear the railway at home, even though it was half a mile away. It was a place to visit and offered me stability and pleasure until I was old enough to harness it properly, to become another Metro-man; someone who used the railway to travel from the edge of the countryside to only partly desirable jobs in London.

You may think that there was nothing very exciting in catching a train every weekday morning from Amersham station, where one's companions were often singularly uncompanionable and driven by the rather pathetic need to occupy their usual seat in which they could fully and wordlessly enjoy their newspaper all the way up to town. Any attempt to hijack the seat of a regular traveller was singularly frowned on. This was a ritual in which the tired occupant could ignore everything outside his little square of comfort, just to exist in his own little world for the better part of an hour before emerging to attend a similarly dull desk courtesy of his largely uncaring employer.

I use "his" advisedly because, around this time, they were mostly men, and the ideal envisaged by the creators of Metro-land now seems rather jaded by overbuilding and the daily commute. Yet my interest was not in the packed commuter train but rather the railway itself, where it went off peak, and what opportunities it created before the realities of life set in, together with concerns about how to pay the heating bill or carry out essential repairs.

Also, the English weather played a major factor, as it always does. Despite the "sunlit uplands" of the idyllic Metro-land described in the leaflets, it was just as bad there as it was anywhere else and so, therefore, were the personal discomforts. Metro-land is a curious combination of the practical and a somewhat dreamlike vision of the countryside surrounding the railway, in which the wistful advertising seemed to refer to another century altogether. Especially odd considering that the Metropolitan Railway actually set out to provide a practical solution for modern man as well as providing a significant revenue stream.

Yet there is much to be celebrated, and what I have attempted to achieve in this book is an appreciation of the development of the northwest London suburbs because of a rather canny idea and some extremely thrusting management. The Victorians were known to have produced an incredible number of grand ideas, many of which were responsible for the early success of the country, and who put today's rather feeble managers to shame, leaving aside Brunel's rather showstopping but thoughtless plan to run the south-western line along the coast through Dawlish rather than inland, where it would not be subject to an angry sea. But doubtless that was unwisely done to show off, leaving the public to put up with regular interruptions to the service, made worse by Beeching's removal of any suitable alternative inland route.

Introduction

Metro-land arose from that background, and the speed at which the Metropolitan Railway was constructed was remarkable, given the interruptions caused by the First World War and the ensuing pandemic. It created a new breed of working man to breathe life into the city, rather than the feeble excuse for today's workers who feel they can do a better job by working from home and only turning up at the office a few times a month. It is one of my greatest annoyances to hear kids and a dog in the background to my telephone call. Call that professional? You may think otherwise; that shipping millions of people back and forth from London each working day was an enormously wasteful procedure, clogging up the roads and the railways alike. It was actually about discipline, originally learned at school, forcing the hapless worker to concentrate only on his employer's needs. And for quite a while it worked: the latter part of the 20th century was generally quite productive. It is only since the dawn of the new century that dissatisfaction and disillusionment have set in, accompanied by a frightening amount of violent crime.

But let's put the clock back, ignore the present and take a close look at how it all began. My focus is inevitably on a particular area, because that is where I lived and what I came to understand. Other regions, no doubt, have their own stories to tell, but this is my take on Metro-land.

⁂

I think probably I was a little too young to reap the full benefits of Metro-land. We were already beginning to enter a period when rapid technological change pushed away the old certainties, and the formality and politeness which I grew up with was already fading, to be replaced by something rougher, where only the more ruthless survived and where consideration and respect, so important during and after the war years, began to disappear. This change is most obvious in British films and television prior to the early 60s, some of which now seems laughably twee in the way people address each other. However, I want to unashamedly recreate for the reader a picture of the past decorated with both history and personal reminiscences. By the time I was born, the concept of Metro-land was already 80 years old, but I was still fortunate enough to benefit from what it had to offer. As with all history, the signs and artefacts are still there to be uncovered, but this book's intention is to recreate the golden age of Metro-land.

You may never have heard of it, because it applies to a relatively limited area north-west of London, and it was never marked on a map.

I make no apology for including apparently anecdotal and seemingly trivial events; they are only here to enhance the history with a glimpse of what it was actually like to live there. So indulge me if you will: I hope you enjoy the journey.

Where is Metro-land? Sometimes spelt without a hyphen, a precise definition is difficult. One definition is the building land that borders the Metropolitan Line, but I do not see it in such inclusive terms. The further you go into London, the more the term loses meaning as the line intercepts and runs parallel with other railways. The big smoke does not encourage that term despite the presence of the Met in central London. To me, Metro-land has more genteel connotations, with the outer suburbs of north-west London and beyond into Hertfordshire and Buckinghamshire. It is not simply confined to property. There may be an strong element of suburbia close to the line, but there must also be green spaces where nature takes over, and large (even very large) properties with gardens and swimming pools. The further the line extends into the Buckinghamshire countryside, the wider the possibilities, simply because there is more countryside.

The other problem in defining Metro-land is the Met's notorious reputation for shapeshifting. Some of the lines that once fell under its auspices are now either run under other banners or simply don't exist at all. An example of this is Verney Junction, its furthest outpost, beyond Aylesbury and 50 miles from London, but today disused. The Met, always the most ambitious of underground lines under Sir Edward Watkin, today terminates at Amersham.

Metro-land benefited from problems elsewhere. Economic difficulties in the north pushed builders towards the south, providing ready-made labour to assist in the construction of new properties along the railway line.

The following extract from Metropolitan Railway literature seems to sum it up nicely.

> Metro-land is a country with elastic boundaries which each visitor can draw for himself as Stevenson drew his map of *Treasure Island*. It lies mainly in Bucks, but choice fragments of Middlesex and Hertfordshire may be annexed at pleasure. As much of the countryside as you can comfortably cover on foot from one Metropolitan Railway station to

another you may add to your private and individual map of Metro-land. (Edwards and Pilgram, 6, 1986)

This description, rather ridiculously, suggests that Metro-land is a kind of promised land for those with the wherewithal to take advantage of it. But promised lands, like Palestine, never quite fulfil that promise because of the natural human tendency to ruin them.

You will note a strong emphasis on the personal. I have been unable to directly reference the above, but I suspect the emphasis on Bucks takes in the original terminus of Verney Junction, since cancelled. The literature goes on in what might be described as purple prose to describe a topography as ideal and unsullied as the Pilgrim Fathers' concept of the New World. It seems to want to create a latter-day quintessential English Garden of Eden complete with "fields which still laugh with golden corn", though the corn may be more in the writing than the reality. This is further confirmed by the following.

> Metro-land is a country of hills and valleys, ridges and hollows, with a few broad plateaus.
>
> Go where you will, the landscape is well farmed, the eye ranges from wood to wood, from tower to steeple.
>
> This is a good parcel of English soil on which to build a home and take root… the new settlement of Metro-land proceeds apace, the new colonists thrive again. (6, 1986)

Almost suggesting that Metro-land is a new country, the literature then goes on to emphasise, in more prosaic style, that whatever style of house you choose,

> you will readily find it in Metro-land – the glorious countryside easily and quickly reached by the Metropolitan Railway. The train service is frequent; the season ticket rates are low, the Educational facilities are excellent, and local golf courses both numerous and good. (6, 1986)

One is left with the feeling that this is largely aimed at a male audience, as it would have been at the beginning of the 20th century, with the little woman left at home to cook and clean, and be satisfied with shopping and having coffee mornings with the neighbours.

So, despite its imprecise location, there is an element of romance about the term, rooted as it is in a 50s Englishness complete with local bobbies and a sense that you were in a relatively safe haven akin to A. A. Milne's Hundred Acre Wood. It certainly formed a strong part of my youth, but does it still exist, or is it just a construct of the past? I make no apology for setting this book mainly in the past because it helps in both understanding the line and my place in Metro-land. I want to convey to the reader what made it special and such an important part of my childhood. The birth of the Metropolitan Line way back in the 1860s was entwined with the rise of Metro-land, even though this came later, and I explain why in this book.

But while the Metropolitan Line itself is a piece of realism that represented a bold modernistic approach to suburban travel, the literature accompanying it, especially with regard to property, is firmly rooted in a previous century; a golden past rooted more in the imagination than in reality, similar in tone to the "sunlit uplands" promised by politicians that are never actually achieved. Yet unlike the unaccountable politicians, Metro-land did produce some real benefits for the first half of the 20th century, in which Keir Starmer's laughable concept of "the working man" aspired to a better standard of living after the horrors of world war. It is just that its reality was simply not that of the quasi poets of the early literature, whose descriptions of Metro-land now seem laughably comic, closer to the unthreatening nature of children's books. Rupert Bear would have felt at home.

The story of the Metropolitan Line is a long and complicated one and now, 162 years on, I am delighted to have witnessed a small part of it. Despite the fact that it was an underground line, it was the very essence of railway building in this country, and should be set against the current disaster that is HS2, with its ruination of the Buckinghamshire countryside. The critic might argue that HS2 is only finishing what the Metropolitan started, but I don't see it that way. The house building along the Met was more measured, an expression of post-war success under better government. I would even say that just as the Met *made* my childhood, HS2 has done its best to *destroy* certain elements of it, especially in its rape of the Chiltern Hills. HS2 is one of the worst decisions in a series of incompetent governments, in which only the locals and the taxpayer have suffered, while the politicians, there one minute and gone the next, render themselves entirely without accountability. The bill is gigantic, billions of pounds and ever rising; in the meantime the damage to the countryside is irreparable. The outcome, if there ever is one, will be pathetic in terms of time-saving, and ill thought out in the sense that it will achieve nothing but harm in an electronic age where

Introduction

so much travel is rendered unnecessary by video conferencing. What should have been done, an upgrade to the Chiltern Line and a refurbishment of part of the old Great Central, has been completely ignored. As usual, the taxpayer gets to foot the bill and nobody is taken to task. For a country that once did so much to promote the railways, it is the most utter shambles. Enough.

This book is not solely a history of the Metropolitan Line, although there is an element of that. In providing an account of the route and surrounds that made up the Met, it reveals that its success was small scale in comparison to the gradual loss of Empire. My aim also is to provide an account of places in Metro-land that were important to my childhood and, in doing so, explain why, for me at least, it is, or was, such a special area. Its birth may have coincided with the decline of Empire, but it also saw the growth of "Little England": the bowler hats and the newspapers, the same seat on the same train every morning. I did it all; well, without the bowler hat, which I decided early on simply didn't fit, in any sense.

Along the way we will take in the construction of a railway line, one which slowly gathered quite a reputation for punching above its weight and gave other main lines a run for their money. It almost became a friend because it was always there for me, something I could rely on when other things let me down. In a world which I couldn't quite control, to either mine or others' satisfaction, the railway became a fallback position, offering, like the coast, a place to forget my problems.

However, in my formative years, I soon realised that the Met's growth and mine were, for a while, bound up together. Like the line itself, there were quite a few diversions which I have found hard to resist. So I have interspersed this appreciation of Metro-land with some of my own experiences to help illustrate its appeal. I may be a product of suburbia but I was not in any way limited to it. My father was not a typical Metro-land householder, especially since he preferred his large Rover car to the train and was as distant from me as any father could be, in close imitation of parent–child relations belonging to an earlier era.

Because the origins of the Metropolitan Line are so complicated, I hope you will enjoy the chance to understand how it all came about , and there are a few surprises. The railways were instrumental in bringing success to this country, even though we now appear to have forgotten everything that we learned. Just as our great architecture is now a thing of the past, so our railways have suffered from continual short-sighted decisions, endless strikes and a stunning lack of management, both

Tracks: A Journey Through Metro-Land

at company and government level. The efficient Chiltern Line out of Marylebone, originally under the German ownership of Deutsche Bahn and part of the Great Central, runs alongside the Metropolitan for much of its length, even partly sharing its tracks. The big bosses who live on its route may be part of the reason why the Met has always been a cut above other underground lines. In turn, it makes the destruction wrought by HS2 seem so wholly unnecessary.

SMALL BEGINNINGS

My first remembered experience in Metro-land was at the age of four when I was taken to the barber's shop near the station. The appropriately named Mr Curley who ran the establishment placed a board across the seat, and I sat on this with my feet on the cloth-covered chair. I think it cost my parents two shillings and sixpence in those pre-decimal days, but somehow that removal of my childish locks established my own place in Metro-land for the next twenty years.

We had just moved from Acton to Northwood, a modern-day Nutwood, in Middlesex. All was new and different. Boots had a book-lovers' library and the local outfitters, French, sold the appropriately dull-grey school uniform. Everything for school had a name tag attached, though why anyone would want to nick a school uniform was beyond my comprehension since they all looked the same and came from the same source. I became a boy from the north woods, with which I had an empathy. It was only people and their demands that confused me. The expectation that your life should follow a prescribed pattern briefly encapsulated as birth, school, perhaps university, work, retirement, death, does not seem appropriate for everyone and could possibly lead to disappointment. I know several people from university who got a first and yet ended up in menial jobs; one simply parking cars. Growing up takes longer for some than others and I always admired the ability of most girls to get to grips with the rigid system from an early age. But my fascination with railways started equally early.

As a child I was given a Hornby Dublo railway set and, having reasonable space to do so, I set up a double-tracked system and marvelled at the detail which went into these early locomotives, steam engines whose days in real life were, both literally and figuratively, numbered. I acquired other pieces of infrastructure like bridges, stations and tunnels to make it more realistic, but of course it was nothing to rival the quasi-realism of today's model railway displays, whose attention to detail creates another world straight out of 1950s England. I was particularly pleased with a toy garage, complete with lift, where cars could be hoisted by a simple lever from ground level for rooftop parking, a forerunner of today's multi storey.

13

I am amazed by the skill and hard work that goes into modern exhibitions, where, in the best of them, a complete new world is created, dominated, of course, by the railway. The stations are remarkably realistic, complete with footbridges, signal boxes and passengers, all in miniature. Alongside are other railway ephemera: tunnels, bridges and sidings. One exhibition even included an aeroplane that actually took off. All that was missing was Noddy in his little car. It is comforting to know that such toys, if such they can be called, appeal right across the age groups, proving that the child is father of the man. Enid Blyton would have loved it. Yet it only seems to emphasise what we have lost. The vision that goes into the exhibitions is almost entirely missing from the real world, except in one respect.

While so many man-made structures are ugly and objectionable, the railway steam engine has always been a joy, as witnessed by the more than a hundred heritage lines dotted round the country. Despite being a massive and intrinsically polluting monstrosity, there is an inbuilt romance to the steam railways which, in these difficult and threatening times, is something to take pleasure in. The countless volunteers who support these heritage groups not only satisfy themselves but give pleasure to thousands. The joy of standing on Dunster station on the West Somerset Line is like going back in time. Its supply of hot drinks and railway ephemera, such as working lamps and models, is a delight, combined with the sound of ancient but meticulously restored steam engines on the 23 miles of track from Minehead to Bishops Lideard. And there are plans afoot to connect it to the main line at Taunton. But this book is only incidentally concerned with steam-hauled trains as, in its early days, they comprised all the Met's rolling stock before a much-needed electrification took over.

Growing up in Northwood, I was ideally placed to watch the gradual modernisation of the Met/GC line from steam and partly electric to fully electric and diesel. Northwood is a suburb some 15 miles or so from London in the county then known as Middlesex. You might have thought that the county name had been specially invented by Keir Starmer to cope with all those of uncertain gender of which we have heard so much in the press in recent times. But actually the name Middlesex is much older, referring to the ancient homeland of the Middle Saxons, similar to Essex (the East Saxons), Sussex (the South) and Wessex (the West). Remarkably, the county name can be traced as far back as the ninth or tenth century, although today it survives only ceremonially as part of Greater London. I am one of the remaining survivors of Middlesex before the county was abolished in 1965. It was also the Middlesex Regiment who were largely responsible for thrashing Napoleon in the Peninsula War. However not even the suggestion of a Middlesex can beat the wonderfully named Hugh Sexey Church Middle School in Wedmore, Somerset, which has nothing to do with the Saxons and everything to do with a royal auditor from Shakespeare's time. Although I am not sure why the need was felt to preserve the name all those years later, especially when it inevitably led to much modern-day ridicule.

When I first acquired a bicycle, I can remember pedalling round the then quiet roads on the outer limits of Middlesex where it joined Hertfordshire. Middlesex always seemed to me appropriately named; sandwiched between the country and the town and essentially middle class in nature. An inbuilt snobbery at that time meant, for example, that the gardener was called by his job title rather than his name, and the daily women, or the women who did, were referred to as Mrs or Miss. Everyone knew their place it seemed; except me, and I am still trying to work it out.

But my interest was not really in cycling through Northwood, rather dull and far too busy and hilly, but in the open roads of Moor Park, achieved by crossing the boundary of Batchworth Lane. As I did so, I began to imagine that I was a train stopping at stations, in my case a selection of kerbside stops outside the more expensive houses that dominated the Moor Park estate, the dropped kerbs denoting the ends of the platforms. One of the stupidities of which was that it had a barrier only at its furthest, Rickmansworth end, where a somewhat officious man in uniform did his best to justify his existence by preventing access to as many people as he could, demanding to know the reason for their encroachment. At the Northwood end there was no such obstacle, giving illicit visitors like me a free run through the private roads edging the now multi-million-pound houses. I knew few people in Moor Park apart from those who went to my prep school, and the high hedges and gates protected the well-heeled from incursions by their less-well-off neighbours from outside the estate. If you wanted to see the big trains you had to cycle all the way to Carpenders Park on the main Midland (Euston) line, a journey of some length and quite a few hills so I rarely did it. But if you made the effort you would be rewarded by some excitingly fast running steam expresses and the vast Deltic, a new blue diesel locomotive, forerunner of things to come and the end of steam.

My route was pretty much the same every time, passing Moor Park station and the few shops nearby. Moor Park, fortunately, lacked a centre so that when you alighted from the train you already felt country-fied, that you had thrown off the dust from town. In those days trains were manned not only by a driver but also a guard with a green flag who stepped out of his compartment to signal the driver to move off. On one occasion on the old wooden platform at Moor Park, the guard, ready to restart, moved away from his compartment to wave his flag at the driver, and the train started to gather pace. Before the guard could regain his compartment he tripped over a suitcase left by a careless passenger on the platform. Unable to regain his composure quickly enough, the train moved on to Rickmansworth without him, the driver none the wiser. It would have been interesting to picture the scene when his loss was eventually discovered.

Edwards and Pilgram tell us that

> In 1923 Sandy Lodge [station] was renamed Moor Park and Sandy Lodge [the name harking back to Cardinal Wolsey's nearby home, the Castle of the More]. The great classical mansion had been sold by the Ebury family to Lord Leverhulme whose Unilever Property Department offered admirable sites in the park for building the house of one's dreams. (76, 1986)

And indeed there has always been something rather special about Moor Park, an island in a sea of relatively unremarkable suburbia. It has always been somewhat snooty but deservedly so because almost every house on this wealthy estate has been carefully designed and kept well apart from its neighbour, this entirely integrated sense of purpose a far cry from most planning these days. However, the advertising for these new properties was more than a touch disingenuous in trying to make would-be purchasers feel good.

> "When world conditions compel the advisability of living economically" the rich businessmen were advised, "the problem which arises is where one can reside and yet retrench whilst maintaining a standard of comfort in a healthy and congenial environment? Moor Park solves this problem!" (76, 1986)

So much flannel to try to disguise the unacceptability to some of being wealthy and not "living economically", and then doing a smart about-turn to describe its intrinsic benefits anyway.

> Distinctive houses from £1900 freehold [the top end of the scale in those days], private roads with a gatekeeper to prevent day trippers roaring through on motor cycle combinations or stop street sellers shouting

their wares, Moor Park was the most luxurious of all the Metro-land estates. "Here one may enjoy quietude and seclusion (without isolation) in the amenities of residence in an old English Park, yet without the responsibilities of ownership." (76, 1986)

Not sure about that last bit since it ceased to be a park a long time ago, and surely all houses carry responsibilities.

But certainly by now the flannel was wringing wet. Of course, Northwood too had some wealthier sections, including Eastbury Avenue, but the wealth was not so extensive. I remember one family that moved there from the rather less chic but still perfectly acceptable neighbourhood in which we lived, enabling them to look down on us without actually saying so. Well, Eastbury Avenue was on a hill. They had made it, but somehow we had not. Did this worry me? Not in the least, and some of those large houses behind high laurel hedges could be awfully lonely places, with their echoing, empty rooms and endless damp gardens. We were invited for Christmas parties involving treasure hunts, and on these occasions the various rooms came into their own.

In later years I began to realise that the freehold label to any property does not in any way guarantee permanence, and we are mere custodians in our time there. What we think we own can disappear swiftly with the onset of unexpected illness, bankruptcy and death, forcing us to reconsider what is really important. Still, I enjoyed the archery lessons in Eastbury Avenue and began to see myself as a latter-day Robin Hood (like Richard Greene on our black-and-white television) but without the robberies, although I had a few local nominations for the evil Sheriff of Nottingham.

On the other side of the railway was Sandy Lodge Golf Club to which, for a time, I later belonged. But it was a poor relation to Moor Park Golf Club, whose clubhouse must rank as one of the finest in the country. The lodge house to this fine 1720 Palladian property stands aloof and alone to the side of Batchworth Heath. Strangely, the lodge somehow appeared in the film *Genevieve* (1954), allegedly situated on the road from London to Brighton in this tale of vintage car racing with John Gregson, Kay Kendall and Kenneth More. But, as with all cinema, it was just smoke and mirrors. W. A. G. Kemp tells us that Batchworth Heath was once part of Northwood.

> A hundred years ago Ducks Hill Road ended at Park Farm, and an ancient lane joined the farm to Rickmansworth Road. In the census

> returns of 1841 Daniel Norton is recorded as living at Home Farm. He was a farmer and timber merchant. (1955)

I remember Home Farm from my childhood before a new estate was built. Situated on the edge of Batchworth Heath, it lay dilapidated and depressed, fronted by a stagnant pond filled with broken tree branches. It hadn't been lived in for years. Its windows were broken and its atmosphere sour. Indeed, it resembled most people's idea of a haunted house. Totally disused, it lingered on for many years and I used to imagine that I could see something moving inside, behind the window panes. Nature was well advanced in reclaiming the space.

Yet just a few hundred yards away was the busy main road to Rickmansworth. Hollywood films about the future (for example *Twelve Monkeys*, 1995) often portray it not as a bright, shiny place where everything works super efficiently, but as a run-down society where everything is broken, the houses are full of weeds and scavenging animals roam the streets. I feel this might be nearer to the truth. Home Farm was the very antithesis of Metro-land, reminding us all that human intervention can only make a relatively small and temporary dent, like the world's abandoned cities. Home Farm then was this in microcosm, until eventually the site was dug up and repurposed for new housing. As to whether you can totally lay the ghosts of bygone eras by rebuilding, I have some doubts.

Kemp goes on to tell us that Mr G. Cornwall, the Rickmansworth historian, has this to say about the Heath.

> It was once common land within the manor of Batchworth, which is said to have been given by King Offa [whatever his real name was] in 780 to the abbot and monks of St Albans. The old manor house which stood at the bottom of the hill has long fallen into decay and modern houses stand on its site. (64, 1955)

Clearly an Offa you cannot refuse. The wonderful entrance to Moor Park was apparently built by the Marquis of Westminster. Close to this is Ye Old Greene Manne public house.

> It is said that [the highwayman] Dick Turpin once escaped through a window at the rear of "Ye Olde Greene Manne", Batchworth Heath. The Bow Street Runners were seeking him at the front of the house. (64, 1955)

The pub has been there since 1728, initially under landlord Richard Ryder and remaining with his family for the rest of the century. There was once a blacksmith's next door, which makes sense for those breaking their journey on Batchworth Heath. Alfred Hodgkison, one of the original blacksmiths, was known, according to his relative, as the Strong Man of Hertfordshire. Apparently he used to drive up to the local turnpike, unhitch his pony from the trap and carry it through to avoid paying the toll.

The Heath was a game preserve belonging to Lord Ebury until the end of the nineteenth century. It was also the scene of an unpleasant incident between a group from the smoke bent on trouble (who had presumably used the Met to get there) and the locals. The wrong sort of passenger.

About 1890 a crowd of Londoners attempted to upset the villagers by throwing clumps of grass into the well and interfering with the drawers themselves. There was a cricket match on at the time and the cricketers declared war on the Londoners. (65, 1955)

A pitched battle resulted in which a number of people got laid out, including Mr Gristwood, a relative of the aforementioned blacksmith, who suffered concussion after being hit by a piece of coconut. The skirmish was only brought to an end by the arrival of the police, who eventually punished the wrongdoers. Thereafter, Batchworth Heath became notorious as the site of this sudden and ill-tempered conflict.

Kemp also mentions the nearby Mad Bess Wood. Bess, the wife of a gamekeeper, used to patrol the woods at all hours of the night, keeping an eye out for poachers. A fierce lady, she was at least her husband's equal in dealing with them. Hence the name, probably dating from 1769.

Moor Park Golf Club, with its massive membership fees, grand decorations and *trompe l'oeil*, is sometimes mistaken for the site of Cardinal Wolsey's (1473–1530) home and, while he undoubtedly made use of the park, his property is no longer in existence. Wolsey, according to Kemp, lived in the medieval building known as the Castle of the More which stood about one-third of a mile north-east of the present building. All that remains of it is the site and the moat. (26, 1955)

That site became part of Moor Park Farm and then Merchant Taylors' School. Henry VIII visited Wolsey when he was still in favour, accompanied on separate occasions by K(or even C)atherine of Aragon and Catherine Howard. But, like so many of Henry's close associates, that favour did not last for long. There is still a Wolsey Road in Moor Park, but unless you are familiar with *Wolf Hall* (BBC, 2016 and 2024), its significance may be lost.

Wolsey's downfall and the ensuing dissolution of the monasteries in the mid-16th century marked the end of Catholic dominance in England. Dissolution is a rather euphemistic term for what turned out to be the systematic plundering of the buildings, their contents and any money available. Much of the stone taken from the monasteries was used for buildings and fortifications elsewhere. More appropriately, I think we can apply the word dissolution to the king himself, one of whose basic concerns was to legitimise his ever more desperate and short-lived marriages in order to secure an heir. Helping him in this was Thomas Cromwell, far too sympathetically depicted in *Wolf Hall*. As a fixer for the monarch, he must have been at least as ruthless as Henry. So Metro-land, in this area at least, had quite a pedigree long before the arrival of the Met Line, although it skirted Moor Park to reach Rickmansworth over fairly level terrain.

The point about cycling through Moor Park was that, even then, I was aware of a special significance to the area, even if I didn't fully understand why that was. It always seemed a cut above the more prosaic Northwood. As soon as you crossed Batchworth Lane you were out of suburbia and on the edge of the country. It was also a move from suburban Middlesex into leafy Hertfordshire, a move which the Met Line visionaries took great pride in. As the Met's construction and associated house building took place, it had the effect of pushing the countryside further and further away from London, even though the literature made great play of the ease with which the train could transport you to an idyllic green space.

I am grateful to the Moor Park Arts Society article *Moor Park Mansion* for the following information about the property. The house that now forms the golf club is mostly associated with the Grosvenor family. The original foundations were laid in the 1680s by the Duke of Monmouth, the illegitimate son of Charles II, the original brick building since replaced by Benjamin Haskins Styles, a Wiltshire country gentleman who made his money from a profitable investment in the South Sea Company. The plans were overseen by Sir James Thornhill, using the theme of Apollo, the sun god. However, the *trompe-l'oeil* designs were developed by Italian plasterers and Giacomo Amiconi, based on the story of Jupiter. Robert Adam designed much of the furnishings which, sadly, have mostly been dispersed across the globe. However, the fine painting of sea gods by Cipriani remains in the dining room.

The East India Company produced the next owner in 1785, Thomas Bates Rous, a merchant trader. We might today describe him as an asset stripper since he demolished part of the building in order to cash in on the valuable stonework.

In 1800 the property fell to Robert Williams, founder of the Williams Deacon bank, long since swallowed up by the Royal Bank of Scotland. He passed the house on to his son, who continued the banking and property connection.

So, after many short tenures, the property was then sold to the Grosvenor family in 1826 where it remained for over 90 years under the Barons Ebury. However, you would have to return to the more mundane Northwood, and its churchyard, to find their burial place, there being no church or appropriate resting place in Moor Park. According to Kemp (27, 1955), the grave of Norman de L'Aigle Grosvenor (d. 1898 aged just 53) is adorned with a beautiful tablet designed by his wife. It depicts an angel with drawn sword standing at a door, presumably the entrance to the afterlife. There is something rather touching about this, given how early he was taken from her.

The station at Sandy Lodge was renamed Moor Park and Sandy Lodge in 1923, thus switching the emphasis to both sides of the railway.

After the First World War the estate was sold to Lord Leverhulme, the soap magnate, and thence to Three Rivers Council in 1937, when it was leased to Moor Park Golf Club on the basis that its 300 acres would help preserve the Green Belt. It is perhaps one of the finest and most ostentatious properties in Metro-land, although there are other contenders.

> The great classical mansion had been sold by the Ebury family to Lord Leverhulme whose Unilever Property Department offered admirable sites in the park for building the house of one's dreams. The mansion and part of the land became the world famous golf course. And few British courses could have a more sumptuous "19th hole" than this. (Edwards and Pilgram, 76, 1986)

I remember the introduction of the Bob Hope Golf Classic in the 1960s, in which famous politicians and actors joined forces annually for a celebrity tournament like no other. The influx of wealthy Americans together with their money added a certain charisma. I remember seeing Gerald Ford and actors James Garner and Ronnie Corbett, to name but a few. It offered a delightful day out for the spectator. I am not sure what happened to the finances but it only ran for a few years, and memorabilia from the tournament found its way into some of the tattier shops on the Euston Road. Yet despite this, Moor Park Golf Club has maintained its allure for those with the money to support it. I was never a very good golfer, unlike my father who won several cups, including a hole in one. Besides, at the time I lacked the income to pay for such luxury.

The idea of the local railway being part of my life was instilled in me from an early age, perhaps because of its apparent permanence. Other things changed as I grew up but the railway was always there, initially as an idle joy and then as a means to get to work. I often wandered through the strip of woodland between the railway south of Moor Park and the road. Once, some friends and I set up a sort of camp there, in the days before parents became unduly concerned about what was happening to their children. It may seem odd today but we were safe, occupying a space that tipped its hat to Christopher Robin and the Hundred Acre Wood, though in animal terms there was little there other than squirrels and the odd fox. Incredibly I was allowed to take a 2-2 air rifle with me. Fortunately I never shot anybody. Every so often a train passed by, reminding us that we were not far from civilisation. Looking back on it, it was excellent that we were allowed to infiltrate the countryside, to discover the world around us and to develop new interests. It was all about developing the person and creating individuality.

I was several miles from home and there were no mobile phones to keep in touch with one's parents, yet I never felt at risk. Things are very different today and it simply wouldn't be permitted. Understandably so, because successive weak governments have failed to stop the rise in crime, and the stabbing of both adults and children has become relatively commonplace. I know it is easy to look back on the past as a golden era, to falsify memories when there was a great deal wrong. Yet that world was indubitably safer, providing children with the means to explore rather than being constrained by screens and meaningless messages as now, and where the risk is both physical and mental due to the hijacking of mobiles by those with criminal intent. I believe that this draws children away from some of the things that really matter, like the land, as emphasised by D. H. Lawrence, although without the need for Lady Chatterley.

I attended St Martin's Preparatory School, just round the corner from me. The school first opened in 1922 with just three boys in one room in a house in Sandy Lodge Way, Northwood. It was founded by the late headmaster, Lionel W. Woodroffe, a veteran of the Royal Marines and Gallipoli (Kemp, 88, 1955). It then moved to extensive grounds in Moor Park Road, to which I could gain access via the footpath at the end of my garden. One day on this footpath I came across a couple of large brown snakes curled up together. Not being of the English variety, I naturally gave them a wide berth. A Dalmatian dog would leap out behind me and put its paws on my then inadequate shoulders. Every morning you had to touch your hat as you went past the head's window, and woe betide you if you didn't. The school's purpose was to prepare boys for public school admission. Every day in assembly the maths master, Mr Wigham, clearly bored out of his skull, made faces at the boys while the Head was pompously addressing them. In the manner of the time it was all very stiff and formal, and stepping out of line might bring about a beating.

It is quite extraordinary that, even in the middle of the 20th century, the slightest diversion from what was deemed acceptable behaviour warranted such severe punishment, without any investigation into its justification or even the consideration of an alternative. Since most of the teachers there were male and the normal practice was to respond "Yes, sir" when one's name was called on the register, I once made the understandable but cardinal error of responding to the French teacher, a Mrs Lummis, in a similar manner and then realising my mistake. Despite my protestations, I was sent out to stand ignobly in the corridor in the hope that I would not be spotted by the Head and more severely dealt with. Looking back on it, I think that she was the one who should have been punished, for being a lumbering baggage with a very inadequate knowledge of French. She was not my idea of a French mistress in any sense of the words. But then many of the best teachers had been cut down in the war, and schools at that time faced a period of inadequate staffing. One of them, an elderly man called Mr Hudson, seemed to gain an unreasonable pleasure from slapping misbehaving pupils on the leg with what became known as a "Huddy stinger". I will say no more.

I doubt if the strong but otherwise roughly hewn wooden box (with nails showing) I was forced to create in what were laughingly called handwork classes and strangely supervised by the elderly Ms Folkes, had much to recommend it, but I did keep it for some years after in a misplaced sense of pride. I also remember sailing my liner on the school pond and noting the appearance of deadly nightshade in the surrounding hedgerows. Always having a passion for dark stories, I idly wondered who should be disposed of. Just in case you have any doubts, I was only eight.

Woodroffe was by now well advanced in years and clearly thinking about retirement. His assistant, a younger red-faced man with a pleasant demeanour, was due to take over. Sadly he became ill and died of a brain tumour before this could happen. And two of my peers were killed in car accidents during my time there; two young lives snuffed out before they even got started. I found this quite shocking, a demonstration that the best-laid plans could go hideously wrong.

These days the school thrives as a trust, and even includes pre-prep nursery schooling, the cost of which can be claimed back together with further incentives for fee reduction as the children get older. It is now subscribed to by a mainly Asian community. The older, largely Conservative voters who lived there when I was a child have disappeared. This may reflect a similar change in other parts of the country, thus partly explaining why the Conservative Party no longer has an audience, along with the lack of trustworthy leaders who understand what being a Conservative is all about. Indeed, there appear to be no political statesmen of any stripe. What is it about Westminster that isolates the MPs who have been elected from those who cast the ballot papers? It's as if the latter no longer matter and now only have nuisance value.

One of the disadvantages of cycling was that you would occasionally be diverted from your course by other people, sometimes in an unwelcome way. One morning an elderly lady stopped me to ask if I had seen her eye. Not quite understanding at my young age, I then realised that her glass eye had fallen out and felt obliged to help her look for it. When it was eventually found in the gutter I hurriedly remounted, just in case she was planning to reinsert it in its current dirty state, which I did not want to observe anyway or be asked to help with it. Hurriedly, I remounted my bike and pushed on only to be stopped again a few minutes later by a man whose wife had clearly left home after a row. "Please ask her to come back." Cycling on, I soon found the escaping spouse, who replied that she was never going back there. I remember hoping that this was not a typical day in Northwood, Middlesex.

I would also mention that my friend Johnny, somewhat disgracefully, managed to override the technology of the time, buttons A & B in the old-style telephone boxes, and used the subsequent free calls to worry a couple of elderly spinster sisters, the Misses Quick, which they certainly weren't. I hope they got over it.

On the same road as St Martin's School was a couple, the husband of which was responsible for giving me my first job, in life assurance in London. He was quite influential and successful in the business, although his background was something of a mystery. Every year he would hold a cocktail party for friends and clients, many of whom were in the acting community. Derek Farr and Muriel Pavlow were but two. This was a great treat for me and that period now seems the very soul of Metro-land: genteel and unthreatening.

Unfortunately, this neighbour smoked himself to an early death, leaving his wife, also a smoker, disconsolate. When you are very young you do not expect things to change drastically but they inevitably do, impermanence being the very stuff of life. A friend of mine who lived further up the road had to put up with watching his father, a doctor no less, deteriorating immediately after retirement from a stroke. He could hear and understand but could no longer speak, because of which some people used to treat him like an imbecile.

One rather lovely girl whom I knew married a boy from St Martin's and swiftly became terrified of him and the rules and regulations he had imposed on her. I was rather surprised at the way things turned out and if it hadn't been for a new baby, she would have upped and gone. I never did find out what happened to her. And so it was that cracks began to appear in what originally had been the supposed certainties of the area.

Another local resident was Jimmy Sangster, not known to many of you perhaps, but actually the power behind many Hammer Films, that bastion of middle-class horror. A writer of some talent, he was responsible for many of the studio's psychological thrillers, for example *Taste of Fear* (1961). He had an ingenious way with twisting normality and was popular in Britain and the USA.

In some ways Hammer showed the flip-side of Metro-land from its base at Bray on the Thames, taking the middle-class ethic and turning it on its head, showing that greed and theft were not confined to the working classes. The plots were often ingenious, though sometimes let down by insufficient budgeting for which Hammer was regularly known. A pirate ship afloat on a local pond was so weakly constructed that the cast fell through the decking. Nevertheless, Hammer has come to be greatly appreciated as a fine British film studio, perhaps more than it deserved, even if they made few productions of any great merit. In horror terms, they led on from the Universal product of the 1930s, only this time with the added incentive of colour and, not forgetting, Peter Cushing. Their origin lies in the period after the Second World War when they started with cheap black and white versions of popular BBC radio programmes like *PC 49* under the name of Exclusive Films and the owner, Sir James Carreras. It always seemed like a family business although, when it collapsed in the 1970s, several only partly successful attempts to revive it were really in name only. Its identity as a purveyor of middle-class horror was never satisfactorily revived.

Another preparatory school in Northwood was rather inappropriately known as Terry's, which I only remember because of some completely unconnected and rather fine boxes of dark chocolates by the same name which my parents often obtained. Although officially the Northwood Preparatory School, Francis John Terry was the founder of this establishment in 1910, a little earlier than St Martin's and just prior to the First World War, which undoubtedly hampered its development. Kemp advises that

> The School building in Eastbury Road, close to the County boundary [Middlesex/Herts], dates from 1912. At that time Eastbury Road ended at the County boundary. In 1929 the road was extended to join Batchworth Lane. Mr Terry bought the School Playing Fields on the Hertfordshire side. (88, 1955)

It had started life in a church – St John's – as did so many of Northwood's establishments, thus emphasising its religious background. After Terry died the school became a limited company, with Terry's widow and the next headmaster, a Mr Riddall, as directors. Then, in 1955, it metamorphosed into an Educational Trust as Northwood Preparatory School Trust (Terry's) Ltd. I was aware of the school but never had much to do with it or its pupils. It seemed curiously detached from my life in Northwood. However, more recently, in 2015, it was absorbed into Merchant Taylors' as its preparatory branch, solving the future problems of both schools in one fell swoop. Actually more than one. Its present location is Moor Farm, none other than the original site of Cardinal Wolsey's The Manor of the More, and therefore rich in history. According to the school blurb

> The architectural remains lie preserved under the sports' fields. Although not mentioned in the Domesday Book, it is known to have been among the manors in south-west Hertfordshire given by King Offa to the abbey of St Albans at its foundation in 793... A peace treaty between England and France was signed here in 1525. (2025)

It seems odd to me that the remains were not properly excavated and then preserved rather than lying under a sports' field. After all, Wolsey was an important man and this is an important historical site. The unworthy thought crosses my mind that perhaps this was because of his Catholicism which, even now, is felt best forgotten in some quarters.

Better to have the thump of Protestant football boots sealing this patch of history and keeping it hidden from view.

The original Grade II listed farm buildings make up part of the school, and plans for a sports hall are underway. So Mr Terry, who died in 1935, would probably have been very proud that from its modest beginnings in a church hall, his creation is now associated with a leading public school. Preparation indeed.

In 1955 there was also another form of education, the Northwood Boys' Club, later St John's Boys' Club, which started in 1913. Along with an emphasis on physical fitness, it had a very strong basis in religion and included a Sunday afternoon Bible class. Teachers from the local schools gave up their time to assist, and although the club had a bumpy ride in terms of suitable premises, it has lasted over a hundred years, developing children's spiritual as well as physical and mental capabilities.

There is no question that Northwood was a local leader in terms of forward-thinking education but I realise that I have barely scratched the surface. What strikes me as most important at this time, in addition to the fundaments of education, was the indoctrination of respect for others, supported by a strong background of religious teaching. Like flood waters that have recently receded, all that is left of this now are isolated pools as the country draws back from specified religion in schools and religion in general, in favour of rampant commercialism and the false notion that pupils should be allowed to think what they like, religiously speaking, without indoctrination of any kind. Does all this have a bearing on the success of Metro-land? I rather think it does because the creation of Metro-land encouraged these communities in the first place and, in Northwood in particular, very successfully.

Unfortunately, because life never stands still, there was nothing to protect Metro-land against the ravages of the 21st century; you could argue that the initial success has been frittered away by both over-development and an almost universal change of personal outlook. Certainly that sense of care for others, encapsulated in respect, has largely disappeared, and to hell with anyone else. Meanwhile, the current Labour government seems set on a path to ensure you can never grab a nest egg in the first place and, if you are somehow lucky enough to do so, they will tax you through the nose as a penalty.

As Orwell predicted: all the animals are equal but some are more equal than others. Crime, once strictly dealt with, is now often overlooked. The Prince is requiring (in taxes) and the judge is forgiving (letting off or feebly punishing major crime). My point is that the simple founding principles of Metro-land may have been lost because, once started, these developments could not be stopped. The level of unchallenged immigration has undoubtedly contributed to that. It is argued that we need the immigrants to carry out the menial tasks that the inherent population do not want to soil their hands with. I would counter that by saying if there were not so many people jammed in such a small country, then there would be no need for many of these tasks to be performed in the first place. It is also the reason why my pictures of Metro-land can only be a series of snapshots of the past, of a time and place as I remember it. Change is ever present, shifting our past pleasures into memories.

Another example of the upright nature of Northwood, with its emphasis on character building with a religious anchor, is recalled by Kemp in one of the pleasant memories of Northwood in the 1920s, so soon after the war and even sooner after the pandemic of Spanish flu that followed it. It took the form of uniting all the schools in the area to celebrate Empire Day and Armistice Day each year. Of course, Empire is now a dirty word to some people, so that celebration has been quietly shelved, especially in the light of so many countries seeking independence.

> Every 24th May they gathered in the grounds of the college and every 11th November they gathered round the War memorial.
> In these united services the Heads of the schools demonstrated that they had one common purpose – to give a sound religious training. This was considered of paramount importance as the foundation of life. (85, 1955)

All the heads of the schools then apparently supported this, and the idea of setting an example as a sure foundation for the life ahead. Kemp comments on how fortunate Northwood was in having so many heads of school with such a deep religious faith. It harks back to the time before the Church gradually lost its meaning and influence on the populace and even, it seems, to many of the people that run it. Justin Welby anyone? How different it was from today's more iconoclastic approach.

The other thing one notices then is the removal of the quality of respect at all levels, something that has almost completely died out in favour of a false admiration for the latest pop stars and footballers, together with an unhealthy obsession with their private lives. The aforementioned heads were the influencers of their time, while the so-called influencers of today are to be found largely scraping the bottom of the barrel on mindless irrelevancies. Why we should offer them any respect is beyond my comprehension. But since respect has now seemingly become irrevocably confused with money, the results are unsurprising.

Northwood at the time of my tenure was a relatively genteel suburb without much scandal, though I do remember two doctors in a local practice swapping wives on a permanent basis. Whether this was carried out without anaesthetic I am unable to say.

The town, nominally overseen by Coastal Command, was relatively affluent. There were the Flemings for example, who had three children: Nicholas Peter, a son who went to St Martin's with me, and two daughters, Kate and Lucy, the latter becoming a well-known actress. I remember going to their house on a couple of occasions without realising that the parents were none other than Peter Fleming (Ian's brother) the explorer and Celia Johnson from Noël Coward and David Lean's *Brief Encounter* (1945). When the other star, Trevor Howard, turned up at the première party, nobody recognised him and he failed to gain admission. A brief encounter indeed.

In the late 1960s some of my friends and I used to meet regularly on a Saturday in the Bluebird Café close to the railway bridge in Northwood. It was a fairly twee venue with beige drapes and an owner who didn't really approve of us, even though we all came from respectable backgrounds with parents who had just about enough money to manage in this fairly conservative suburb. No, Mrs Bluebird's objection was based on age and potential rowdiness. She wanted adults of a certain age who would bring a particular aura to the proceedings. She never actually chucked us out but she would have liked to. But then this was in the era before coffee bars with music had really caught hold, where we might otherwise have ended up. In isolation we are nobody and we only really establish our identity by mixing with others to find common ground and interests. There were no mobile phones to distract us and I for one was rather glad of it. We were not forcibly warped by a mindset of screens and followers, and the pressures that come with them. It seems now a very innocent and necessary escape from one's parents who, let's face it, were probably glad to get rid of us for a few hours. It was all a world away from today, but possibly more natural and healthier. After all, what could have been more boring that having to attend meals and coffee mornings with parents' elderly friends and fake aunts?

One elderly couple only visited occasionally, thank goodness. Ernest and Freda Bristoll had to come out from Acton where my parents originally lived, and they could have come straight out of the 1930s, with his car that occasionally needed cranking and a smart dark-grey suit accompanied by a pocket watch and handkerchief. His wife was rather plump and whiskery and they were both ineffably boring. Just hearing that they were coming to visit was enough to put me into a coma followed by a need to find an escape route from Stalag Gruff I.

A similarly dull couple lived along the Met route at Northwick Park. The Lymes were probably ideal Met candidates, entirely happy with their suburban lot near the railway. Their house was as unremarkable as they were, and even if it had been entirely empty for the whole of their tenure, I doubt it would have made a great deal of difference to anyone around them. They were well named: I nominated them as having Lymes disease – as far away from *The Third Man* as you could imagine. Yet these were the people my parents mixed with, and my father, a very passable golfer, can be seen in business photographs enjoying slap-up dinners with other similarly attired penguins and a few well-known golfers of the time. There is a photo of him with the once famous Henry Longhurst.

The annual fortnight holiday away from Metro-land was no better, although I found some pleasure in the Great Southern Hotel in Parknasilla, Éire, where it was then possible to bring the lift back down from an upper floor without the upwardly bound passengers being able to disembark. This was achieved by keeping one's finger on the lift button in the lounge and then retiring to an armchair behind a newspaper to observe the resulting annoyance and bewilderment. I was once able to do this three times without being spotted. and before the guests were able to exit the lift. I think the hotel is still there, but by now I should imagine they have found a way to fix the lift.

However, being out in a boat with an outboard motor weaving its way between granite cliffs and thousands of sea birds on the edge of the Atlantic was another pleasure, especially when the local dolphins, always up for a game, swam alongside us as a kind of escort. There we met the Tussaud family of Baker Street waxwork fame. Colloquially known as "the two sods", Angelo was actually a charming man, gentle and kind, who did not deserve his hard-nosed wife. Eventually she left him and I heard that even on his deathbed, for he was considerably older than her, she had apparently refused to visit him. Perhaps there was a place for her in her own museum.

Northwood was remarkably self contained, having convenient train and bus connections, the latter served by a Green Line coach, together with some good schools. Even Merchant Taylors', for the boys, was not far away. The various denominations were adequately catered for, although Holy Trinity, the Protestant parish church, didn't get my vote for the following reason. The vicar of the time was a red-faced man, well on in his eighties, who when confronted with my mother seeking help after the death of my father refused to offer any on the basis that he was a Catholic. Instead he flew into a rage about the deficiencies of the Catholic Church, leaving her in tears when she had come for practical consolation.

The priest then in charge of the Catholic church was also rather understandably severe, having worked on the Burma Railway and suffered accordingly. On one occasion, in the midst of sermonising from the pulpit, he instructed a lady with a screaming child to leave the church because the congregation "could not listen to both of us". Much embarrassed, she did so, but it could have been dealt with more sympathetically. The priest, obviously a damaged individual who I think had been whipped, died young.

Neither example shows religion in its best light and one can understand how some turned away from it. Nowadays, it is hard to understand what C of E actually stands for; when a character in a television drama did not know what to do with his dead colleague because of his apparent lack of religion, another chimed in that, in that case, he must be C of E. An all-purpose religious collecting bowl, especially nowadays, without any apparent distinction.

At one time the churches used to rail against bad decision-making by the government. Now you don't hear a peep from any of them. They are too concerned about frightening the horses. And when one Catholic luminary actually made an effort, he was besmirched with claims that his behaviour fell far short of what was expected, and he was forced to leave the Church. Even the sermons are now quite bland, designed to fill up a quarter of an hour rather than deal with the problems of the age. So the sting, along with the power, of religious life in England seems to have disappeared just as our politicians no longer seem able to discriminate between right and wrong.

Thus we continue on, rudderless, with one weak government after another where the politicians feather their nests with freebies while steadfastly ignoring the people who voted for them. There are no longer any leaders, just anodyne jobsworths. It is also the reason why the country's railways suffer appallingly through lack of management. Just take a look at France to see the difference, despite their moribund economy. Even in the north-west, in Brittany, not perhaps the most important area, France boasts a number of efficient high-speed trains. And it is not all down to the relative lack of space here. We have opportunities but rarely take them, preferring to sink into bureaucracy, as if that were a solution. To run a railway you need the vision of the Victorians, and at least we seem to be gradually waking up to the need to revisit some of Beeching's more crass decisions, even if, at the time, there were too many loss-making branch lines. Hope springs eternal.

In considering Northwood as a centre of Metro-land, I should also include Mount Vernon Hospital, important to me for two reasons; first because my father died there following a car accident, and second because we obtained our family cat there, chosen from all those roaming the grounds. My mother taught Sooty to beg for his food while the rest of us managed to obtain it without the need to do so. Kemp tells us that the hospital

> stands high at the top of Kewferry Hill, a fine view from many parts of the district. It opened in September, 1904, as Country Branch of the North London Consumption Hospital. [How that dates it.] The opening was performed by Princess Christian, accompanied by a bodyguard of cavalry. (83, 1955)

Incidentally, she (1846–1923) was the third daughter of Queen Victoria and Prince Albert, becoming Princess Christian of Schleswig-Holstein by marrying an impoverished German prince. According to Kemp

> In 1929 it was decided to convert the Hospital into a centre for the treatment and investigation of malignant disease.
>
> The Hospital was converted into a General Hospital in 1939. This was under the Emergency Hospital Scheme, and after the war it was decided it should continue to function as a General Hospital.
>
> It now contains [in 1955] 250 beds for general medical and surgical cases, 120 beds for the treatment of patients by radiotherapy, and 120 beds for plastic surgery. [All pretty small by today's standards.]
>
> In addition, the Hospital has all the departments necessary to a large modern general hospital as well as a large research department and its own School of Nursing. (83, 1955)

To start with, the hospital seems to have suffered from an identity crisis, no doubt made worse by the constraints of two world wars. Today it is part of the Hillingdon Hospitals NHS Foundation Trust, with a state-of-the-art Cancer Centre and new facilities planned. All this has come with Northwood's transformation from a genteel suburb to a busy suburban hub, helped immeasurably on its way by the development of the Met. Northwood today is surely part of Greater London, which it surely wasn't in my childhood.

In addition to Mount Vernon there was, in 1955, St Vincent's Orthopaedic Hospital, on Haste Hill, nearer Ruislip and Eastcote.

> In front of the main building a broad slope faces directly south. On this stand the open air wards providing a magnificent view for the patients. Harrow church spire, and on clear days the Hogs Back in Surrey are plainly seen. (83, 1955)

The hospital aimed to prevent crippling disease with the then-modern open-air treatment of children and adults. A sort of sanatorium. Today, the hospital buildings have been demolished to make way for St Vincent's Nursing Home. It is run under the auspices of the Sisters of Charity of St Vincent de Paul, with more than three quarters of the original 18 acres having been sold off. Today, it looks after dementia cases and physical cases, and offers palliative care for those at the end of their lives. Both now and in its original form it strikes me as highly vocational.

And then there was RAF Coastal Command, in my youth a bastion of official protection but also a likely target for enemy bombers. At the time I knew little about it although, rather ridiculously as it seems now, I believed it to offer safety for the good citizens of Northwood, though in fact its net was countrywide rather than local. A hangover perhaps from the Second World War, but as we now know, we are never safe. In fact, from its Operations Room in Eastbury Park, it played a vital role in tracking the movements of enemy aircraft and shipping, including U-boats. And knowledge, as we know, is power, enabling the formation of suitable strategies to counter any perceived threats to our country. Originally based at Lee-on-Solent, Coastal Command moved to Northwood in 1939 as the magnitude of Hitler's threat became clear.

> During the Second World War, Coastal Command's most important contribution was the protection of Allied convoys from attacks by the U-boats of the German Kriegsmarine. It also protected Allied shipping

from aerial attacks by the Luftwaffe. The main operations of Coastal Command were defensive, defending supply lines in the battle for the Atlantic, as well as the Mediterranean, Middle East, and African theatres. (Wikipedia, 2025)

Northwood was not its only base, and it had representation in other countries such as Iceland, Gibraltar, the Soviet Union and parts of Africa. With the aid of substantial investments, it was able to track and destroy U-boats with increased efficiency, though most people now remember it for the destruction of the *Bismarck*. With what national pride the country once carried out these tasks.

After the war, there was a rapid reduction in Coastal Command's services, although it played a significant role in the Cold War. It was also involved in the Berlin Airlift of 1948 when the Soviets attempted to cut off aid to the city, which was jointly occupied by the major powers. By the 1950s, its aim was to track any possible Soviet threats, and although this is still very much the case, Coastal Command was closed down in November 1969. So, had I but known it, I witnessed its dying days, before its duties were passed to other squadrons.

The Command had been deemed too expensive to maintain in peacetime but, as we know, governments of any stripe have been severely lacking in their duty to respect a primary requirement of government; to protect their citizens against enemy incursion. You would have thought that a Conservative administration, looking back at the war, would have learned the importance of that, but both them and the Labour Party seem to regard defence as of only secondary if not tertiary importance. Thus, dangerously, the funds are not there. War, as Putin demonstrates, is about posturing as well as action, and it is easy to see why Russia regards the West as weak. Nowadays, of course, you don't need enemy bombers to destroy the West: simply taking out the internet would be enough to incapacitate large sections of the community, as we have periodically seen.

The reason I have been concentrating so much on Northwood is not because I think it was better than many of the other suburban developments along the Met but because, growing up there, I knew it best and much of what could be found there was fairly typical of other towns in the area. There were no great buildings or cathedrals and, admittedly it was totally lacking in style compared to larger towns such as Bath or Chester. But the interest, the devil if you like, is in the detail, and while the Met never turned out to be a grand line connecting the great cities of the land, you could be forgiven for thinking this might be the case when you consider Edward Watkin's original plans. It is interesting to note that his wilder flights of fancy, like the Wembley tower and the Channel tunnel, all eventually had to be ignored, leaving, nevertheless, a highly successful queen of the underground.

Northwood is where I learned to be me, although it took me some time to establish my confidence in what became an increasingly competitive society. I was always on the periphery, observing the game, and it was only later I was able to put those observations to good use. In the same way, despite a number of false starts, it took the Met a number of years to become fully encapsulated in semi-permanent form. The Stanmore branch and the extension out to Verney Junction were just two of these later irrelevancies.

The town of my childhood also had the Northwood Literary Society. According to W. A. G. Kemp it

> flourished from about 1905 until after the First World War. Held in Emmanuel Church Hall every other Friday evening between October and March, the meetings were very popular. Packed audiences used to enjoy listening to eminent speakers and writers and authorities. Great naturalists and explorers held their lectures illustrated with lantern slides. (97, 1955)

I don't think David Attenborough was there but he might have been.

> In the days when there was no "wireless" and no lights in the Northwood streets, Friday night was an extra special night for anyone with a respect for culture… Once John Masefield came and read his poems. Another time St John Ervine talked about the novel. With his Irish wit he kept us in roars of laughter. G K Chesterton gave one of his inimitable talks. (97, 1955)

The Rev. C. F. Ayerst called the first meeting in October 1905, and presumably it provided a welcome distraction during the horrors of the First World War. There were a dozen people on the Committee and no doubt the NLS provided an opportunity to meet the famous literary icons of the day, even if political and religious discussion was deliberately excluded.

The appeal of the Met Line is best explained in a few examples. When you arrived home at Northwood station, where the town played host to St Helen's School (founder, Miss Rowland Brown) and Northwood College, you felt you had finally left the smoke behind. To confirm this it was easy enough to quickly cross the high street and leave the town behind by taking a footpath that ran alongside the railway, skirting the backs of houses before eventually leading to that most English of pastimes: some allotments that also bordered the railway. To get back to my house you had to cross a wooden footbridge, since replaced by a metal monstrosity, and that occasionally offered its own magic.

It was possible to get out from the bottom of our garden in Grove Road and access a wooded footpath that bordered a farmer's field once owned by a Mr Campion, a relation of Gerald Campion who played Billy Bunter of Greyfriars School on television, ever dipping his hand into a regular supply of appealing buns, whether they belonged to him or not. Essentially middle class, this in turn reflected the area in which I found myself; a safe footpath on which you could eventually reach the town centre without taking to the streets. You only needed to cross one road before rejoining the footpath which led to the aforementioned railway bridge.

The bridge stood about half a mile outside Northwood station, which you could not see because it was just hidden by a curve in the track. So although you might not have been able to see trains from far off, you could certainly hear them. The thing to do was to access the bridge just when it began to get dark, at a time when one of the GC steam express trains was due from Marylebone. These tracks were then not just for the sole use of the Met Line but were shared for a time with steam trains on the Great Central line, two of which were named express trains: *The South Yorkshireman* and *The Master Cutler*. The names indicated their final destination in Yorkshire, and particularly Sheffield. Designed to run towards the Midland Railway connection at Bletchley, they were a remarkable sight in my childhood, named expresses steaming along an essentially suburban line. Named expresses reflected the pride that British Rail once had in their services, but those days are long gone.

As a child the anticipation was everything, but I don't think it would be very different now. These important trains would first make themselves felt with both the sound of their pistons and the smoke rising from their chimneys some time before they came into view. You had to position yourself in exactly the right place on the footbridge so that the approaching steam engine, perhaps with twelve coaches, would drench you in steam as it passed underneath the bridge; you temporarily lost your vision as the steam flecked with flame enveloped you. It was strangely cleansing. With the steam creeping up from between the wooden slats you could stand and watch the trains approaching from either direction. These passenger trains, each one running once a day in each direction, ran fast to Aylesbury but sometimes had to contend with being stuck behind Met Line trains stopping at every station. What, you might ask, were these beauties doing, muddled up with suburban traffic, crawling through suburban stations such as North Harrow, Pinner and Northwood? The answer is complicated.

Great Central trains out of Marylebone had their own non-electrified tracks until Harrow, with a branch at Neasden taking some stock out towards High Wycombe. Up until the early 1960s there was only one set of tracks in each direction between Harrow and Aylesbury and both the Met and the Great Central had to share them. This led to substantial overcrowding and late running, so something had to be done. I remember a pink leaflet being delivered to all houses in the affected areas, announcing a one-million-pound modernisation scheme (how far would that go now?), doubling the tracks between Harrow and Rickmansworth, thus easing the congestion on the present system. Those trains taking the new, outer tracks would thus avoid the suburban stations between these two points, enabling improved speeds and journey times. But the outer tracks were not confined to the Great Central trains, as a number of Met trains could also take advantage and run fast between Harrow and Moor Park.

However, the days of steam were even then numbered and the spectre of Dr Beeching began to loom above the horizon. So the Metropolitan was inevitably linked to the Great Central. By the time Beeching closed the Great Central down in the 1960s, it had only been open a mere 67 years. It is now plain to see that this was a considerable error, due to population growth and HS2. Of course, part of it was taken over by the Chiltern Line which now runs an efficient service from Marylebone to Aylesbury.

Unlike the late comedian, Tony Hancock, who could not see the appeal of railways – "three hundred people hurtling through the rain" – for me at a very young age, they had a strange appeal, the polished tracks promising to take you to distant blue remembered hills where ghostly figures replayed childhood games over and over. This feeling is perhaps shared by the volunteers who run the many heritage lines throughout the country. We used to lead the world with our fine railways. Sadly we seem to have forgotten almost everything we learned, especially in terms of management.

But, for now, I lived in my own private world, one to which I would often retreat in later years. Northwood (originally Northwod or Northwode), Middlesex, was a crossroads in the late 1950s. Unlike its neighbour, Ruislip, it had relatively little important history. The only house of real note was The Grange. According to Kemp (15, 1955), it may have been a rest house for monks.

This came about because it was owned by the monks of Bec-Helloin Abbey in Normandy and had connections to Ogbourne Priory in Wiltshire. A building by the back door was held to be the monks' chapel, adorned at one time by a foliated cross. Appropriately, the house was taken over by the London College of Divinity in the late 1950s. Northwood started life as a parcel of land, a spin-off from Ruislip originally owned, surprisingly, by King's College, Cambridge. I hope you are beginning to see the connections remaining from the Norman invasion of 1066; William the Conqueror, Duke of Normandy, did not speak English, and neither did some members of the monarchy that followed him. We had become inevitably bound up with Europe even then and in particularly France. We didn't need a Channel tunnel to create a link, it was already there through the Norman conquest of England and our later conquest of part of France. A visit to Fontainebleau Abbey will reveal the tombs of many "English" monarchs of the time.

A Dr Nash and his wife lived at The Grange in 1934; according to one of her letters, she saw the ghost of a monk, and so vivid was her account that all the maids refused to work there and left. The Grange was occupied from at least as early as the 14th century and probably well before, as the Abbot of Bec leased the house at an annual rent of five marks to a John St George and his wife, on the basis that they would keep the house in good condition. Since then there have been many architectural additions. Being the oldest in the area, Kemp quite reasonably holds that the house can make a claim to be the origin of Northwood: Roque's map of 1754 shows the name Northwood assigned to the site. Dr Nash was responsible for bringing a 15th-century screen of gold and scarlet colourings to The Grange, which he purchased from a church in London. A fine house indeed; it may not be as ostentatious as the mansion at Moor Park, but according to Kemp, workmen have found interesting artefacts there at various times, including a half-groat of Henry VI (originally from Calais) and a 1604 shilling, not to mention Cromwellian clay pipes.

At this point we should mention Northwood Hills, today an unremarkable suburban adjunct to Northwood and completely without the charm of the much older Pinner. As my photograph of 1931 shows, the Joel Street bridge became the site of the new station and the country lane transitioned into a double parade of shops complete with an art deco cinema round the corner. The sign on the bridge in the photograph announces that

> Metropolitan and Great Central Joint Committee Site for new station. Frequent train services will run to London, City and West End. (1931)

Edwards and Pilgram tell us that

> Northwood Hills was largely a joint creation of a building estate developer called Peachey and the Metropolitan Railway. The Met made Peachey agree to cover any losses the new station might incur in the early years of his estate. But so popular was the area and so rapidly did it grow, that this stipulation was soon withdrawn. The station opened in 1933 and was almost the last of C W Clarke's "domestic style" buildings for the Metropolitan. (73, 1986)

I wish I could be more enthusiastic about Northwood Hills. It seems to entirely lack character in favour of the purely functional. It may have to be considered part of Metro-land, but it would definitely not be included in my own personal map, being rather too colourless to qualify.

A relatively unremarkable, but genteel conservative town in the 1960s, Northwood faced in two directions, largely due to the presence of the Metropolitan Railway. To the south-east was an ever-increasing suburbia; to the north-west the countryside and the Chiltern Hills. This transition from town to country was undoubtedly part of its appeal for me. The old brown electric trains that made up the rolling stock had brass-handled coaches on which were proudly inscribed *Live in Metroland*. But what exactly did that mean? There were many underground lines operated by London Transport, so why was this one special? That is largely the purpose of this book. The Metropolitan's place as the uncrowned king of the underground lines ran right through my childhood, and even now, living far away, it still leaves a strong legacy.

Moving on, I think it appropriate to run through the birth pangs of the Metropolitan Line so that you can understand exactly how Metroland grew up around it.

A BRIEF HISTORY OF THE METROPOLITAN LINE

In order to fully understand the design of Metro-land, it is necessary to go back as far as the mid-1800s, to the original seeding of the Met's origins. The following is a brief outline of the history of the Metropolitan Railway. It is not intended to be exhaustive for two reasons. Firstly, because it has already been covered in depth by other more skilled transport writers, and secondly, because this book is principally about a secondary effect of the line, the birth, growth and points of interest of Metro-land.

The Met overcame a number of extraordinary difficulties before it became the railway line we know today, not least because of two world wars and a number of economic and practical problems that were overcome by the skill and determination of its instigators, even if it took a few wrong turnings along the way. These consisted of early attempts to take in other underground lines, which eventually proved to be not a natural organic part of its growth and were eventually abandoned or ceded to other companies. Despite the shapeshifting, the growth of the Met describes the realisation of tremendous Victorian ambition, even if its early years as a London steam underground were shrouded in difficulty. But the determination of its founders, and particularly Sir Edward Watkin, makes for an intriguing story, as does the solutions required to solve the fundamental problems that dogged the birth of the line.

The Metropolitan Line is, at the time of writing, 162 years old, and we should perhaps compare this with the sad demise of the Great Central, open for a mere 67 years, a remarkably short period for a mainline service and, as it turned out, with the increase in population and the advent of the disastrous HS2, remarkably short-sighted. Betjeman's "beechy Bucks" became Beeching saving bucks. But more on that later.

It is also good to know that the Met's current directors are very conscious of its history and that of the Great Central. As such, regular celebrations are held in which fine old locomotives are brought out of retirement to the enormous pleasure of the attendees. The skill, dedication and attention to detail brought about in these restorations is wonderful to behold.

But not only steam. For me, there is no finer sound than the mournful whine of the Bo-Bo electric locomotives that pulled Met trains to Rickmansworth. Whatever I happened to be doing, it brought my mind back to the Met in an instant. I shall never forget it. There are still one or two left of these distinct, maroon-painted locomotives in operation, all of which were named after important people of the then recent past like actress Sarah Siddons or John Lyon of Harrow School. Their engine note, a plaintiff whine, seemed to herald something special to me. They were a largely unsung triumph of the Met. If you get a chance to see one, don't turn it down.

We need to think of the Metropolitan Line as just one of many bold ideas of Victorian visionaries. The men who planned it seemed to be very aware of the deficiencies of London life and what was needed to improve it. At the time, the City needed an injection of both funds and people to turn it into an important business centre.

The Met was originally much longer than it is now, stretching all the way from Aldgate, where it shared tracks with the Circle Line, to, incredibly, Verney Junction in Buckinghamshire, some 50 miles from central London, where it even provided an intersection with the once deceased but partly restored Oxford and Cambridge Line. Much of this development was due to the influential landowners of the time, some of whom wanted their own private halts. So before its current route was established, the Met was also responsible for other lines such as the Stanmore branch, which we now know as the Jubilee. We need to keep in mind the part played by major landowners in shaping the line, especially at the outer limits of the project.

According to Mike Horne

> Matters were steered by a local enterprise called the Aylesbury and Buckingham Railway (ABR). The ABR was created by an Act of incorporation of August 1860 with the object of providing a direct line between Claydon and Aylesbury... The promoters already had the support of Sir Harry Verney, one of the major landowners in the area: the other big landowner was the Marquis of Chandos and in order to engage his support a new route was identified passing Quainton Hill to the south-west and serving more effectively the Marquis's estate at

> Wotton. In return the Marquis contributed £5000 and volunteered to become chairman – Sir Harry became deputy chairman. (10, 2003)

Claydon House, incidentally, was the ancestral home of the Verney family, although it is now owned by the National Trust and there is a small museum attached. If Moor Park is perhaps the finest house in Metro-land, Claydon House runs it a close second in terms of interior design. Set in a rural haven, close to water, the estate was presumably a deer park originally. The house was built in the mid-18th century; close by is All Saints' parish church, peeping out of the woodland. An elderly Florence Nightingale was supposed to have stayed there, at a time when she needed nursing. It may be fairly plain on the outside but the inside is a joy of exotic design, the Chinese Room being of particular interest. A coffee shop is close by for those who want to while away a sunny Sunday. The house, although in the Aylesbury Vale rather than Wessex, made an appearance in the 2013 film version of Thomas Hardy's *Far From the Madding Crowd*, presumably for its exotic interiors.

For an underground line to have such grand ambitions was amazing, even though it was first scaled back to Aylesbury, and then to Amersham, where it terminates today. The discarded stations on the route were taken over by the Great Central and, when that closed, the Chiltern Line, which terminates at Aylesbury. A further stop has recently been introduced at Aylesbury Vale Parkway, reflecting the increased population, and the odd special is occasionally trundled up the old GC track at very low speed to Quainton Road. Somehow the Great Central has refused to die completely, despite the iron fist of Dr Beeching.

According to *A Brief History of the Metropolitan Line* (2023), Charles Pearson first suggested a London underground railway in 1845, backed up by another plan from John Williams. Pearson's idea was to build an "atmospheric railway", in which a pressure difference drives a car along like a pea in a pea-shooter.

It sounds like an early version of the Japanese bullet train. Charles Pearson was a London lawyer, solicitor to the Corporation of London and, briefly, a Liberal Party politician. According to Wikipedia, "He campaigned against corruption in jury selection, for penal reform, for the abolition of capital punishment, and for universal suffrage" (2024). To that extent he can be seen as an energetic man of vision with strong ideas ahead of his time, so his concept of an underground railway is not so surprising. Edwards and Pilgram describe its birth as follows:

The Great Western Railway, which had been unable to build its terminus closer to the centre than Paddington, was naturally anxious to carry its passengers all the way into the City. The Board found itself sympathetic to the wishes of the City Fathers who looked for a new railway link with the expanding western suburbs… But in the end it was largely due to Charles Pearson, Solicitor to the Corporation of London, that the successful scheme which became the nucleus of the Metropolitan Railway got off the ground.

Pearson gave freely both of his enthusiasm and his money. "I remember Charles Pearson telling me he had spent £8000 out of his own pocket in placing a Metropolitan railway service before the public," Lord Mayor McArthur said in 1881.

Finally, Pearson persuaded the Corporation to find £200,000 to add to the £175,000 already put up by the Great Western Railway in order to build an underground railway. Ten years were to pass before the work was finished. (11/12, 1986)

It says something about these Victorians that they were happy to set in motion great schemes in which they were small but dynamic cogs, and which were sometimes unlikely to be completed in their own lifetimes. So there was an unspoken generosity of spirit here (almost entirely lacking in today's breed), in which the country would be the ultimate beneficiary rather than them personally.

John Williams further developed the idea of an underground railway because it would reduce the amount of traffic on the streets. Pearson's plans to link Farringdon to King's Cross in 1852 came to nought, but these were part of the birth pangs of the Met Line. Pearson's company was bought out, but his plans were developed so that the line would be further extended to Paddington. Two years later, in 1854, the North Metropolitan Railway Act was passed allowing construction to begin. However, more detail was needed to make it viable and several years elapsed before sufficient capital was available to start work. Construction did not in fact begin until 1860, on one of only two underground lines to breach the Greater London perimeter.

According to *A Brief History of the Metropolitan Line* (2023), three accidents occurred before much work had been done. The first involved a small boy of eight who slipped and fell under a passing bus whilst playing on the spoil near King's Cross. Sadly he did not survive. In the second incident, a train on the Great Northern Railway failed to brake at King's Cross, overshot and fell into the newly dug Metropolitan Line works. Surprisingly there were no deaths but some injuries, and blame fell on a drunken guard who had failed to apply the brakes. The third involved a boiler explosion on a workers' locomotive, again near King's Cross. Two men were killed. All of these accidents occurred in 1860; not a very auspicious start, yet deaths were possibly inevitable on a project as far reaching as this one. The railways have a long history of accidental deaths amongst its navvies, especially when it came to building tunnels.

As a footnote to this it is worth recording that in May 1862, James Driscoll became the first man to be killed on an underground railway following a violent dispute with a colleague, Edward Gregory, who flung him with great force into the cutting below, breaking both his legs. Whilst Driscoll did not die directly of his injuries, the shock of the ensuing amputations finished him off. Gregory was convicted of manslaughter, a remarkably light sentence given the circumstances.

In May 1861 part of a cutting collapsed alongside the Euston Road, causing substantial damage to nearby homes. While this may have looked like shoddy workmanship, it is important to remember that large infrastructure projects such as this are rarely achieved without mishap, and this was partly brought about by inclement weather.

That same year, a number of journalists accompanied the top brass on the world's first recorded journey on an underground railway, in an open-top car between Paddington and Edgware Road. They then walked the tracks to Euston, followed by a short journey from King's Cross to Farringdon and back. The staff included chief engineer John Fowler and Chair W. H. Wilkinson. On 24 May 1862 William Gladstone, then Chancellor of the Exchequer, rode the same tracks, this time all the way from Paddington to Farringdon. He was fortunate because, the following month, the Fleet sewer burst through the cutting after heavy rain, causing considerable damage, thus delaying the official opening of the line by several months until early 1863. At this time the stations involved were Paddington (Bishop's Road), Edgware Road, Baker Street, Portland Road, Gower Street, King's Cross and Farringdon. So, at this time, the Met was strictly a London underground railway, but it was not to remain so for very long.

The grand opening was held on 10 January 1863, and while the stations were largely in the same position as we know them today, a few of them had different names. We also have to remember that this was initially a steam underground line, and therefore extremely unhealthy, sometimes downright dangerous. The risk of boiler explosions and shunting accidents was commonplace, and the railways generally were nowhere near as safe as they are today. You may recall that author Charles Dickens was personally involved in a railway accident brought about by a train being allowed on a track that was undergoing repairs. It is said that he offered assistance to the wounded.

Nearly 40,000 people rode the line on the opening day, travelling from Paddington (Bishop's Road), through Edgware Road, Baker Street, Portland Road (now Great Portland Street), Gower Street, King's Cross and Farringdon Street (now Farringdon). We can see from this that the section from Paddington to Baker Street eventually became part of the Circle Line, while Baker Street became an interchange, with some of the Met trains actually beginning their journey there to the north-western suburbs, while others came through from Aldgate. Baker Street now consists of two curving island platforms so that the two outside bays could be reserved for trains starting or finishing their journey there.

Just 18 months later, in 1864, an extension from Paddington to Hammersmith opened, although this is now part of the Hammersmith and City Line. We can see from this how the Met gradually established its own identity. Nevertheless, things were looking bright for the newly fledged line. In 1865 the Met was extended eastwards to connect up with Aldersgate Street (now Barbican) and Moorgate. According to *A Brief History of the Metropolitan Line*, "Almost a year to the day after opening… contractors working above the tracks manage to drop a four tonne iron girder just as a train is passing below. It smashes through a carriage killing four people. Remarkably the line is up and running again within half an hour" (2023). While feeling for the victims, the rapid restoration of service is remarkable for the time and something we could take a lesson from today.

So in 1865, in what today would be regarded as a remarkably efficient construction programme, the Met extended eastwards into the City, connecting Aldersgate Street (now Barbican) and Moorgate. The City connection was considered a vital one. But there was an initial problem. This rapid and generally successful construction had surprisingly overlooked one thing: the availability of rolling stock. As a result, although the Great Western had lent some of theirs, the various extensions meant there was an overall shortage. So the Met went cap in hand to the Great Northern, who lent some of the early locomotives to supplement the carriages and locomotives provided by the Great Western.

Edwards and Pilgram tell us that

> Fowler, the first Engineer of the Metropolitan, had planned to use locomotives carrying stored steam, but care had been taken when

constructing the underground railway to leave ventilation space to enable steam from the locomotives to escape. The Select Committee of the House of Lords had been told, in 1853, that railway signals would be so obscured by steam and smoke as to be invisible. Immediately the line opened, alarmist paragraphs appeared in the daily papers headed "Choke Damp". To allay public panic, a small fan and an engine were arranged to blow fresh air into Portland Road station, and side glasses were removed from Gower Street station. The early stations had great glass and timber roofs which did not extend to the full length of the platforms. (13, 1986)

If this sounds woefully inadequate, so it turned out to be: "However, in spite of condensing apparatus fitted to the locomotives using the line that was eventually to become the Inner Circle, the atmosphere and tunnel ventilation of the Met proved a constant source of trouble until the introduction of electric power" (13, 1986).

It was bad enough running steam trains above ground, but below it was a recipe for accidents and chronic respiratory problems. Despite their best efforts, the Met did not really solve this problem until the introduction of electrification. In the meantime, the steam locomotives had to be kept in shape. For one thing there had to be a constant supply of coal, only available at certain key stations, Baker Street and Farringdon being two. It was stored in one-hundredweight wicker baskets and placed on the platform opposite where the engine would come to rest. As you might imagine, the job was labour intensive and put in the charge of the coalman who, assisted by the fireman, loaded the fuel into an on-board bunker.

It was one thing running a steam train through a tunnel in the country, but quite another where the entire line was enclosed. As some sort of sop to the difficulties, a bonus was paid to drivers who used the least coal (and presumably, as a result, caused the least pollution). The Metropolitan based the bonus on mileage, the Inner Circle being just over 12 miles in total. Certain drivers became expert in coal economy and thus benefited more than the rest. So the line, in its early days, was a wildly unhealthy place to be, and no doubt regular staff members suffered lifelong lung conditions as a result. There are no figures available to test these theories. Edwards and Pilgram tell us that

> First experiences of travelling on the steam-hauled underground carriages was terrifying. Between stations, passengers inhaled a

noxious mixture of steam, coal smoke, soot and sulphur. Jets of dirt puffed through every small hole around the doors and windows, as one Met traveller remembered. (13, 1986)

Strangely though, there was little in the way of complaints from the public, possibly because it was offset by the novelty of ease of travel through central London. However, the following example gives an idea of just how bad the situation was.

A rather old, lame and stout lady was travelling from Aldersgate Street. Because of her infirmity, she was forced to step down from the train backwards, taking great care. The enthusiastic station staff spotting her in the murk assumed she was boarding and that she had become stuck in the doorway. She was heaved in and "right away" waved. Incredibly, this accident was repeated later, despite her choking pleas… She was almost asphyxiated by the pungent railway fumes and when her plight was finally revealed she had to be rushed to St Mary's Hospital, Paddington. (14, 1986)

However, the board were very much aware of all these endemic problems, but when a doctor suggested the use of large fans in 1881, the Met Chairman of the time was not that keen on spending the money in this way: he was far more interested in extending the line out to Aylesbury. However, ventilation shafts up to street level were eventually dug out, which proved a partial solution to a very serious problem.

Ventilation shafts from the tunnels to the roads can still be seen. They were a practical solution which was made possible by road rebuilding… Newly arrived visitors from the country had no idea what created the huge clouds of steam that often arose from the gratings. (15, 1986)

However, this was no more than a small step in the right direction. In the meantime, the Met had possibly made matters worse by the introduction of gas lamps inside the carriages so that passengers could read. There were, of course, inevitable leakages.

Edwards and Pilgram, quoting A. J. Hearn (128, 1986), tell us that station lighting varied significantly on the Met prior to electrification. Oil lighting was mostly to be found at country stations while others such as Rickmansworth and Pinner favoured gas. While Northwood changed to electricity as early as 1906, many stations on the Met's inner circle were lit by gas until 1912. Guards' signal lamps and train tail lamps could often be replenished by oil.

All in all, travelling on the early underground was a risky business, particularly if you were a regular passenger or staff, particularly drivers and firemen. The effects on their respiratory systems were not all that different from working down a coal mine. Whereas this seems horrifying and wholly unacceptable to us today, it was a stage of development that the early underground inevitably had to go through.

ELECTRIFICATION

Electrification of the line at the beginning of the twentieth century was by no means straightforward and the Met board were forced to consider a number of options before it was finalised. This no doubt came as a considerable relief to the Met's board, given the problems of running steam locomotives underground. Curiously, the site of one of Edward Watkin's failures became an opportunity to test out a form of electrification on the now moribund branch of the failed Wembley tower. Horne tells us that

> Two carriages… were built at Neasden works and these were intended to be equipped with four motors each and a form of series-parallel electrical control. Contractual difficulties surrounded the supply of generating equipment, but makeshift arrangements were put in place involving a withdrawn 4-4-0 locomotive jacked up and connected mechanically to a pair of dynamos by a drive belt. (28, 2003)

While this may sound rather Heath Robinson to us, the effect was apparently quite satisfactory during the experimental period of about a year. The Met was looking at other opportunities however, including the highly successful Ganz system in use in Switzerland on the Lake Como railway. It had in fact been developed in Budapest and as a result, the system, which involved twin overhead wires, was used in a number of countries on the continent. Yet the Met, rather than taking it on, eventually decided to build a power station on its own land near the Neasden works. This was decided upon after considering and then rejecting another site at Edgware Road. Neasden offered the necessary space for development, and what today we call "future proofing".

But going it alone had its own untested difficulties. Ironically,

> Neasden generating station was convenient for coal to be delivered by rail and for water to be obtained from two (three from 1919) deep artesian wells… The plant was supplied by the British Westinghouse

Electric and Manufacturing Company and comprised three (soon four) 3.5MW generators driven by Westinghouse turbines running at 1000 rpm. (29, 2003)

The power was fed to a couple of conductor rails, between and outside the running rails. However, a number of failures with this plant resulted in interrupted electrical supply, and eventually, a series of claims against the manufacturer involving, *inter alia*, the coal-feeding equipment which was producing toxic, sooty and grit-filled smoke. Some years ago an electric train heading southbound towards Southampton was inadvertently diverted onto the non-electrified Salisbury branch at Basingstoke, resulting in red faces all round when the by-now powerless train and its equally powerless driver had to be hauled back into the correct electrified area.

> The long drawn out financial settlement of the claims against the manufacturer included modification of the turbines and rewinding the four generators for 5MW. A fifth turbo-generator was added in 1908 together with six additional boilers, making a total of twenty. (29, 2003)

As a result, the first electric train came into regular passenger use on 1 January 1905, running as a stopping train from Baker Street to Uxbridge. By the end of that year every all-station train on the route was electric, a quite remarkable achievement considering the initial difficulties. As the Uxbridge branch had, for the moment, very few passengers, it was eventually fed with a shuttle service. I will provide more detail on that later.

> Power was conveyed at high tension to substations at Baker Street, Finchley Road, Neasden, Harrow-on-the-Hill and Ruislip, at each of which transformers and multiple 800kW rotary converters (1200kW at Baker Street) reduced the voltage to around 600V dc. At this voltage it was fed to a pair of conductor rails, one centred between the running rails and the other just outside on one side. The above substations comprised generally three converters, though there were four at Neasden and only two at Ruislip. Additional substations were provided on the Met's Inner Circle section. (Horne, 29, 2003)

This is just a brief summary of the technical developments; it is a complex subject and has been explained at length elsewhere by Mike Horne.

> However, despite this difficulty, the trains serving the area north of Baker Street on the main Met line were developing nicely, with new saloon coaches intended for service mainly on the Inner Circle; quite arbitrarily, saloon vehicles came to be referred to as "coaches" rather than "carriages"... Entrances were provided only at the car ends... Accommodation was provided for first and third class passengers... First class accommodation had more elaborate interiors with green leather seats in the smoking saloons and "art green" moquette in non-smoking sections. Bevelled mirrors and photographs of interesting places in areas served by the Met completed the scene. (Horne, 30, 2003)

It is worth noting that there are still craftsmen painstakingly restoring the interiors of railway carriages and the moquette seating to an unbelievably high standard. I take my hat off to them and it is one area where we British still excel.

It is worth pointing out that second class was abolished in 1905, coincidentally the same year that electrification began to be introduced. I can remember the use of "Ladies Only" compartments on Met trains in the 1960s. As a child, and a poor speller, I was initially confused by these which I took to mean Laddies Only. I was soon disabused of this. The eventual removal of these compartments led to some wild and bawdy speculation in subsequent years concerning the present whereabouts of these ladies or, indeed, if they now existed at all.

> Much of the older steam-hauled stock was either disposed of or laid up, but the comparatively new bogie carriages now existed in larger numbers than were required for the infrequent steam trains on the Aylesbury line and were felt worth converting to electric operation. (30, 2003)

In this interim period, there was a mixture of steam-hauled and electric trains, with steam being the preference for trains running beyond Pinner and electric being used from initially Wembley Park and then later Harrow. This meant that passengers would have to change trains partway through their journey if they wished to travel to the outer suburbs. This may seem unsatisfactory but I think was a necessary interim step in development.

The first set of ten electric locomotives were supplied by British Westinghouse. They had a combined output of 800 horsepower, which meant that they were limited to a maximum speed of 36mph on level ground, but were slower still on hills. Unsurprisingly, being new and relatively untried, these gave a certain amount of trouble and eventually had to be modified. They were fitted with Westinghouse air brakes and weighed a whopping 50 tons.

The conversion to electric gave the Met a problem as to what to do with old rolling stock; the Met's stock was also significantly inferior to that being run by the Great Central, with which, you will remember, they shared some track, especially the line north-west of Harrow and onwards towards Buckinghamshire. There were also insufficient motor coaches. Consequently, a decision was taken to modify the first-class 1905 stock into a more modern design of compartmental carriage. As a result the Met was able to create two new loco-hauled trains with a design known as "Dreadnought". This created a train with three third-class and two first-class carriages, with a combined capacity of 314 souls. Deemed a success, four new similar trains were built; equipped with, for the very first time, passenger alarm handles.

From the above we can understand that electrification was inevitably a difficult and troublesome project, either because of the hitherto untried electrical locomotives but also because of the consequent inappropriateness of some of the rolling stock. This was due both to a regular fluctuation caused by keeping up with developments, and also because of the Met's continued commitment to the Inner Circle, something it would later drop. Yet happen it did, even in a period of world war and at a pace that we would consider remarkable even today. In harness with this began another change, this time alongside the track. Horne tells us that

> In the 1880s and 1890s housebuilding proceeded rapidly between Kilburn and Willesden, and a little beyond: to some extent this was fuelled by the Metropolitan's own housebuilding activities on its surplus land, much of which was bought for just this purpose. (32, 2003)

This put the Met in a key position as a seriously important and thrusting company, which made an enormous difference not only to the narrow strip of land on which the line was built but also to the area around it. This became the key to Metro-land. The Met was cannily creating its own passengers as the line pushed outwards through the north-west suburbs. Every time a new station was created or even improved, it usually spurred a building boom in its vicinity. The Met initially favoured a low-cost approach to some of the stations, especially where they were unlikely to have a large footfall. I can remember the original Sandy Lodge/Moor Park station being made up of wooden boards underfoot before it was eventually modernised in the 1960s: the two original wooden platforms were converted into two island platforms when a further set of double tracks were introduced between Harrow and the Watford branch. This in turn created faster journey times and the ability to run more trains instead of one slow, stopping line taking in Northwood, Northwood Hills, Pinner and North Harrow, which were bypassed by the fast line; especially useful in the rush hour.

I hang my head in shame at my lowest day concerning the Met on what started as an ordinary morning at the office. That afternoon I was instructed by my manager to take a colleague from a brokers to lunch as he was likely to be a valuable source of new business. Unfortunately, unlike me, he was insatiable in his demand for alcohol. After a drink-filled two hours at lunch, the pubs were closing, as they did in those days, and I said I should be making moves to return to the office. However, he had other ideas, knowing a club where we could continue drinking unabated. I vaguely remember some underground dive, and even when this had finished and I could barely stand, he then wanted to return to the pubs, which had reopened for the evening session. My office had long since closed. However, never having been any sort of drinker and quite unused to this level of imbibement, I insisted on returning home before I became quite unable to do so. The journey home was exceedingly long drawn out as I had to take a stopping train and get out at many stations en route in order to relieve myself. This made for an enormously protracted journey time of at least double or even treble the usual, because each time I alighted I then had to wait for the next service. In a shocking state for the rest of the evening, I never repeated it.

The Uxbridge branch was initially extremely underused and, as a result, the stations, which had often been set up at the request of pressure groups, were markedly inferior, with wooden platforms and very little shelter from the elements. The stations so affected included West Harrow, Rayners Lane, Ickenham, Eastcote and Ruislip Manor. The take-up was initially so poor that the branch was run as a shuttle service terminating at Harrow rather than the originally planned through trains to Baker Street. But, once again, this was just the beginning, and the first flowerings of Metro-land began to show in some often remarkable Betjemanesque garden estates, with the occasional expensive property dotted along the route. Northwick Park and Hillingdon did not open until 1923, whereas the stations already cited on the Harrow branch had all opened before the First World War.

In the meantime, thanks to Sir Edward Watkin, who was largely responsible for the remarkably swift expansion of the line, plans for growth continued unabated. An extension was initially built to Hammersmith Road, an area that, incredible as it might seem to us today, was "still filled with orchards where early strawberries and soft fruit were urged to early harvest for London tables" (15, 1986). The idea that Hammersmith could be anything other than a suburban monstrosity accompanied by petrol fumes is entirely foreign to us. The line reached Hammersmith in 1864 and Richmond in 1877. This, of course, is no longer part of the Met, one of those early distractions before the line found its true identity in the north-west suburbs. But just as the Met created new opportunities for living, it was inevitably destroying the countryside bordering the line, a countryside that the line's own leaflets held up as an intrinsic part of the project. This, of course, was carefully hidden from Metro-Man, who probably only got to realise it when it was too late.

SIR EDWARD WATKIN

Edward Watkin, largely responsible for much of the Met's construction, was incidentally a relation of my one-time headmaster at Downside School, the studied Dom Aelred Watkin, a monk. It seems an appropriate family transition, from visionary Victorian to monasticism, with its concentration on higher things. But even the monks are gone now, either dead or banished to the outer reaches.

What is truly thought of as the Met, the line into the north-west suburbs, did not begin until 1868. By 1880, a huge programme of construction had taken place, driving the line as far as Harrow-on-the-Hill. For this rapid development we have to thank Edward Watkin, who allowed little to stand in his way. It should be understood that his original masterplan was to grow the Met into a mainline railway, the envy of the other companies. At this time, the line was still under steam traction, and (third rail) electrification, at first partial, did not happen until some years later, in 1905. Apart from dealing quite swiftly with all the aforementioned pollution problems, it also substantially speeded up the service.

Watkin could be a difficult man but there was no denying his drive. He was one of those people who could cut through apparent difficulties with the sharpest of knives and achieve lasting solutions. Eventually he came to see that trying to run the entire Inner Circle, as well as pushing the line further north-west, was just too demanding a task. The Met's primary purpose was to run trains from the suburbs directly into the City, so the southern section of the Inner Circle was eventually deemed irrelevant to the grand plan. This is why the Met eventually shared the northern stations of the line as far as Aldgate with the trains that looped round the Circle. Another distraction disposed of but, in so doing, a superb feeder line directly into the City had been created, which could only be beneficial. Watkin took up chairmanship of the Met in 1872 and set about organising the company's finances on a proper footing (in place of the previously useless bookkeepers) so that further expansion could begin. Amongst his various aims was to inject new blood into the City, thus increasing the importance of London as a financial hub.

Edward Watkin is someone we need to seriously admire because, without him, it is unlikely the Met would ever have become as important and far reaching as it did. This despite the fact that it never became the main line that Watkin originally envisaged. It is undoubtedly true that had he not seen the development of the line in grander terms than was actually achieved, it is unlikely that what we take for granted today would ever have happened.

Edward Watkin (1819–1901) was an MP and railway entrepreneur. According to Wikipedia

> Among his more notable projects were: his expansion of the Metropolitan Railway... the construction of the Great Central Main Line, a purpose built high-speed [for then] railway line; the creation of a pleasure garden and a partially constructed [but ultimately abandoned] iron tower at Wembley [originally conceived to rival the Eiffel Tower in Paris]; and a failed attempt to dig a Channel Tunnel under the English Channel to connect his railway empire to the French rail network. (2025)

According to Edwards and Pilgram

> Watkin was a walking encyclopaedia of railway knowledge and experience. Starting his career in a goods office of the London and North-Western Railway, he became chairman of the South Eastern Railway and of the Manchester, Sheffield and Lincolnshire Railway. He was to be the Metropolitan's Chairman for twenty-two years. It was under Watkin that the Metropolitan began its expansion into the countryside of Middlesex, Buckinghamshire and Hertfordshire... linking the Manchester, Sheffield and Lincolnshire Railway with the South Eastern Railway and the Channel Tunnel. Watkin put his case to Parliament: "If the line is made it will make the Metropolitan and South Eastern parts of a system running right through the country – a sort of backbone for the commerce and industry of the country". (16, 1986)

It was his ultimate inability to achieve a link between the Met and Worcester that turned his ambitions to creating a railway that would run from Manchester to London and onwards to Dover, with the object of connecting to Europe. Incredibly, Watkin actually started digging a Channel tunnel in conjunction with the South-Eastern Railway in 1880, and although it failed because of his inability to convince Parliament, it was probably just as well in the light of the two subsequent world wars. Had it been there then, their outcome might have been very different. In fact, it might have been necessary to blow the thing up in order to prevent an invasion.

I note that we are now being invaded, by immigrants, who take their chance on the high seas and usually have little truck with the tunnel. As a result, far too many lose their lives in the attempt, either in boats or imprisoned in the back of a lorry. Politicians of any stripe seem quite unable to deal with it and, consequently, our already overcrowded island is full to bursting with people, many of whom cannot speak English and, often, do not work. Enoch Powell predicted "rivers of blood" from such an influx but, with the exception of certain isolated incidents, this has not happened. Instead, the very Englishness of the country has withered away. Not all countries have suffered similar fates and France, to name but one, still seems defined by its Frenchness.

Watkin first put shovel to earth at, appropriately, Shakespeare Cliff, between Folkestone and Dover. It reached a length just shy of 1,900 metres. But the project did not carry the population nor indeed Queen Victoria with it. The view was, even then, that the French might use it for an invasion. The image of a French onion seller bicycling into Kent with onions draped over his handlebars and perhaps a few French loaves in his basket comes to mind. So Watkin's project turned out to be a tunnel too far; with both the War Office and certain members of the royal family against it, it never got past first base. Despite Watkin's skill at winning over dignitaries to his point of view, no amount of champagne receptions within the tunnel could get over this hurdle. In this case, he simply hadn't done his homework properly. In addition, and this was the real killer, the concept was blocked by Parliament, and there was no getting over that. You might have thought that it would have been wiser to test the waters, so to speak, before going down this particularly expensive rabbit hole, but this was typical Watkin, an impulsive man who would often push his projects through by sheer willpower. But we should continue to admire him. His visionary far-sightedness is now sadly lacking. You can still see the sealed entrance to Shakespeare Cliff today and it is perhaps ironic to note that the real invasion came via foreign immigrants from France, but they were not French.

Eventually, Watkin, the Liberal MP for Kent, suffered a stroke which took him out of the game altogether. He was never solely allied with one party, his allegiance dependent on support for his ideas rather than political loyalty. For example, despite being a Liberal, he voted against

Gladstone's Home Rule for Ireland bill. He still claimed to be a Liberal, just one that moved away from the mainstream of his party. In truth, there was no clear indicator of his politics and he voted for anyone or anything that might support his projects, which were far more important to him than day-to-day party politics. He was knighted in 1868 in the early days of the Met and became a baronet in 1880. He also became High Sheriff of Cheshire in 1874. Yet, despite the much-advertised failure of his Channel tunnel project and ill-conceived plan for a tower at Wembley – on which more later – Edward Watkin was the main player in the early growth of the Met and important aspects of many other railways.

Watkin's reputation has faded with time, unlike the sustained record of achievements of Isambard Kingdom Brunel, yet his record abroad was equally remarkable, particularly as it ran concurrently with his activities in the UK. For example, Watkin was President of the Grand Trunk Railway of eastern Canada (1862–69), creating the Intercolonial Railway which connected Halifax to Quebec. He was responsible for building the Athens-Piraeus Electric Railways, and was also involved in projects in India and Africa. As we know, he was involved with many of the leading UK railway companies of the time and the wonder is that he was able to juggle all these projects and still achieve results. His reputation was such that, at its peak, it seemed that if you wanted to construct a railway almost anywhere in the world, he was the "go to" person to help get the project off the ground.

Curiously, it was not Watkin's original idea to run a line from London to Aylesbury. Various projects had been mooted from as early as 1845, most of them intended as branches from already existing lines. Watkin made it a reality, although it developed in small stages. In 1868 a single-track line was created from Baker Street to St John's Wood; it was largely underground, so construction was slow going. An extension of this moved on to Swiss Cottage and eventually West Hampstead, but with the addition of double tracking (1879). This might seem a minor step forward, but the line from Finchley Road was now above ground, which meant that further work could be carried out much more quickly and the push through the north-west suburbs could begin. One cannot appreciate just how quickly housing sprung up along this route without reading a couple of contemporary accounts.

> "Amongst the charms of Kilburn is its proximity to the country. Within half an hour's walk the pedestrian is among trees and fields and pleasant places."

"The district about Kingsbury and Neasden is intersected by green lanes and field paths bordered by flowering hawthorn hedges, while the River Brent meanders through them." (16, 1986)

I still wonder how the leafy suburb in which I grew up has changed in such a quietly dramatic way to become a defined part of Greater London. Change is inevitable but the Met was only partly responsible for that. Population growth and immigration are also to blame.

The former quoted account also refers to "the interminable brick and mortar wilderness of London". One wonders what the reaction would be today. So while the concept of Metro-land was essentially a good one, the cynic might say its downside was the destruction of huge swathes of countryside. And it is true, you now have to travel out of London at least as far as Wembley Park before you get little sense at all of green space. But that is also the reason why, for me, Metro-land does not really begin to exist until you get north of Wembley Park. Its concept rightly evokes a strong flavour of the countryside even amongst the new suburban homes, but particularly as you get out into Hertfordshire and Buckinghamshire. It used to be possible to hear the local accent in Chorleywood pubs. Not any more. Sadly the M25 now feels like a circle round Greater London while, during my childhood in Northwood, well inside the ring, there was never any sense of the proximity of London at all.

We should also mention at this point that, in the early years, the Met was responsible for the line out to Stanmore, long since taken over by the Bakerloo (cum Jubilee). There appears to be no reason for this until one realises that the Met, if it were to fulfil its remit as a major line to the suburbs, had no business stopping at interim stations like Swiss Cottage, St John's Wood, the now defunct Marlborough Road, West Hampstead, Kilburn and the rest if any speed to the outer suburbs was to be achieved. So we could look at the Met as the middle of a sandwich between the Great Central, which ran non-stop from Marylebone to Harrow, and the Bakerloo, which stopped at all the interim stations. Eventually, therefore, the Met quite rightly cast off the Stanmore branch so that its trains could run semi-fast from Baker Street or Aldgate to Wembley Park (and sometimes beyond), apart from a pause at Finchley Road at the outer limit of the tunnelled area.

Whilst the Met did not create the concept of suburbia, it did produce a great deal of new suburbs in a ribbon development alongside the various stations. It is celebrated in John Betjeman's film of *Metro-land* (1973, d. Edward Mirzoeff), particularly around Harrow. This post-war picture of the male property owner, travelling by train to work during the week and mowing the lawn and washing his car at the weekend, created an ideal to aspire to. The picture that Betjeman creates is of the working man entirely satisfied with his lot, happy to spend his weekend downtime with menial chores around the house. The concept seems just a little dull now, but makes sense in its post-war context. The reason for that can be found by looking closely at the post-war period. The good citizen, having put his back into helping his country, was now faced with having to look after himself and his family. The bar was set much lower than it is now. We were satisfied with less. After the Second World War, the government set in motion a number of advice forums to help the ex-soldiers get back on their feet. The rampant commercialism that surrounds us now was not there and so the intentional attempt at discomfort that we mistakenly feel if we do not keep up with modern trends was also absent. There was no sense of maximising yourself; only what may seem to us now a rather stifling sense of conformity. However, we should always remember the post-war situation as Britain got back on its feet. Ration books persisted for several years after the war. Money was tight and there were shortages in all areas, not least in property, where so much had been lost to wartime bombs. As a result the idea of continual personal betterment was not as firmly entrenched as it is now. There was, as now, a basic hierarchy of needs, but it meant having a roof over one's head and looking after the family. Vaulting ambition was, for the most part, absent.

   The other aspect of the Met's vision for its Metro-land population was that it was an essentially male version of how life should be lived, with the little woman out of sight and confined to the kitchen, completely out of kilter with female emancipation, where the female rightly expects to be treated on at least an equal footing in terms of jobs, recognition and pay. However, it has taken at least a century since women were granted the vote for this to become a reality, and it could justifiably be argued that it still hasn't been properly achieved, in some companies and far-flung territories. It has been an incredibly long haul from giving women the vote to the current situation where they are still discriminated against in some groups where old habits seem to die extremely hard. Equal pay is often hard won and the decision whether or not to pay is taken, as often as not, mainly by men. But even after the Second World War, it was still possible to see in London's streets in the early 50s signs offering accommodation, yet with the warning that "no Blacks and no Irish" would be accepted. This now seems highly offensive.

If the expansion of the Metropolitan Line fulfils your idea of modernisation, remember too that 26 May 1868 was the final opportunity for crowds to watch a public hanging at Newgate. The people who attended would probably now be found braying at football stadiums, and it seems incredible that pleasure can be drawn from watching others have their lives snuffed out. Yet it is not a million miles away from watching the gladiators of ancient Rome and illustrates the deep-seated sense of barbarism that hangs over us from earlier centuries in all sorts of ways. It now seems confined to watching murders on screens both large and small; I suppose this is a blessing, but the crime rate and the severe nature of much of it shows that not much has changed. This attendance at executions seems an extraordinary juxtaposition of the barbaric old and promising modernity. Authors Charles Dickens and Wilkie Collins, who attended these rituals, were both fascinated and appalled, and it should be remembered that Dickens' own father was, for a while, held in a debtors' prison. What's more, you could take the Met to Farringdon to help ensure you got a ringside seat at these hangings. The trains were steam powered but, in another nod to modernisation, electric traction was on the horizon.

THE RISE OF METRO-LAND

Metro-land (or Metroland, in some spellings) is not officially recorded as a place in any history books or maps and, as I explained earlier, it is impossible to define with any accuracy. But the term is generally taken to mean those suburban areas near the line in Middlesex, Hertfordshire and Buckinghamshire; in other words well outside London. So there is perhaps a certain snob value to the term, coined as early as 1915 by the marketing department of the supposedly independent Metropolitan Railway County Estates Ltd, since the railway company itself was in the privileged position of retaining surplus land which would eventually be developed for housing. This was further confirmed when the *Guide to the Extension Line* became the Metro-land guide. According to this, "It promoted a dream of a modern home in beautiful countryside with a fast railway service to central London until the Met was absorbed into the London Transport Passenger Board in 1933" (2024). This is somewhat misleading since it implies that this aspiration died upon the Met's absorption into the London Passenger Board. Nothing could be further from the truth, since this was only the beginning of what we now understand as Metro-land.

A vital aspect of the growth of Metro-land was how the land surrounding the railway became synonymous with the railway itself. This was due to a lucky break.

> Unlike other railway companies, which were required to dispose of surplus land, the Met was in a privileged position with clauses in its acts allowing it to retain land that it believed was necessary for future railway use. Initially, the surplus land was managed by the Land Committee, made up of Met directors... Robert Selbie, then General Manager... suggested a company be formed to take over from the Surplus Lands Committee to develop estates near the railway. The First World War delayed these plans however, and it was in 1919, with the expectation of a housing boom, before the MRCE was formed. Concerned that Parliament might reconsider the unique position the

Met held, the railway company sought legal advice. The legal opinion was that although the Met had authority to hold land, it had none to develop it, so an independent company was created, although all but one of its directors were also directors of the railway company. The MRCE went on to develop estates at Kingsbury Garden Village near Neasden, Wembley Park, Cecil Park and Grange Estate at Pinner and the Cedars Estate at Rickmansworth and create places such as Harrow Garden Village. (2024)

All this had its origins in the estate cottages built for the Met's workers at Neasden as the line developed. It all sounds a little like the housing provided by entrepreneurs such as Cadbury and Rowntree for their chocolate factory employees. Their lives were carefully wrapped and proscribed, like the chocolates. The remnants of this attitude of ownership of its workers survive at John Lewis today but this is a shadow of its former glory days. The housing envisaged for Metro-land initially suggested independent ownership; yet, at the same time, compliance with the *status quo*. So while we cannot directly compare the Metro-land ethic with a Disney model village, both are underlaid by a sense of propriety and following the rules. John Lewis even supplied holiday locations for its workers so that it could be in control at all times.

It is all a question of levels really and the owners of this new suburbia had much in common, despite the much-vaunted minor differences in their front doors and windows. Certainly the owners of the larger houses in Metro-land would not have thought so much about compliance, but rather what they could achieve individually. For them the Met was just a means to an end, the posh houses to be found in Herts and Bucks offering a privacy behind iron gates and high hedges not available to the toiling suburban Joe. So, like most ideals, the concept of Metro-land was not clear cut but a little fluffy round the edges. Such is the nature of humanity itself. One size will never fit all.

Mike Horne tells us that

> After the First World War the Met was prolific in its publicity and for many years produced a wide range of imaginative posters to promote its services, of which, unfortunately, very few survive. It was famous also for its booklets promoting country walks which started in 1905. These demonstrated that traffic could be generated to remote country stations [as they were then] even if few people lived there; the popularity of such journeys was further increased by means of cheap tickets, such

as walking tour tickets which allowed return from a different station. The Country Walks theme was also adopted by the Met&GC upon whose metals there was perhaps more scope, especially in later years when housebuilding was making "country" walking more difficult in the Met's now built up area. (52, 2003)

The Met also produced a set of maps describing its services, some of which were of a curiously irregular scale, leading to some geographical anomalies such as Golders Green being further north than Watford.

Even more surprising was the railway's superimposition on what looked superficially like an accurate road layout. This was a novel way of dealing with the awkward problem of showing clearly the congested central London at the same time as the wilds of Brill. (53, 2003)

The maps were produced at the same time as those issued by the Underground Group, which understandably confined itself to the London area. Later maps were issued by the Met which, strangely, were limited to the area of electrification and gave no indication that the line ran out to Aylesbury and, originally, well beyond. This was probably partly because of the enormous stretch of the line, while most of the ticket-buying public would have been limited to the more suburban areas. Originally, of course, journey times were longer than they are now and the daily commute to town dictated that the suburban areas were initially preferable.

What Metro-land did offer, in contrast to many other lines, was a sense of pride in itself and a certainty that it could provide what was needed for a good standard of living in the period after the First World War. But how it moved from an incomplete concept to a reality can be crystallised in the British Empire Exhibition of 1924 and 1925, held in close proximity to Wembley Park Station. The Exhibition was also, in some measure, responsible for the growth of Wembley Park and, for me, the beginning of Metro-land. The Metropolitan Line succeeded wonderfully well because it was, for the most part, in the hands of supremely competent managers. It was also helped along by two events at Wembley, the British Empire Exhibition of 1924/5 and the Olympic Games of 1948, and the resulting huge increase in the number of people travelling by train for these events, alighting usefully at Wembley Park. Mike Horne tells us that

The old station building remained largely unaltered from Metropolitan Railway days, but to handle Olympic traffic a new station structure was built alongside, connected by a wide gallery to new stairways halfway along each platform. Although the Olympic ticket hall was never used for everyday traffic, it remained an essential part of the station's ability to cater for the crowds travelling to the Wembley complex for major events. (23, 2003)

While these two events were standouts, there was regularly increased footfall to scheduled events at the stadium. All of this contributed exponentially to the growth of Metro-land and no doubt encouraged others to set up home in other towns along the route. Both Wembley Park and Harrow-on-the-Hill stations underwent a number of changes to cope with the demands of the increased railway traffic.

In the meantime, Agatha Christie and her then husband Archie Christie were given the enviable task of drumming up business for the BEE by travelling to key points of the Empire. At that time Christie was not that well known, having only published one novel. The Empire still covered a vast number of territories, but cracks were, nevertheless, beginning to appear and the Christies, along with certain other ambassadors for the Exhibition, hoped to attract key member states to send representatives to Wembley, to demonstrate their skills and the nature of their country. Unfortunately, the cracks were also appearing in the Christies' marriage; this was perhaps their final time together before Max decided he preferred someone else.

In many cases the BEE presentations were a success, but the result was more like a series of extremely detailed sideshows such as you would see at a grand fair, rather than the intended outcome of firming up the crumbling edifice of a once great Empire. The rot had already set in and the comparison between the thrusting Metropolitan Line and the dwindling Empire in 1924 was marked. So, in a sense, the aims and objectives of the BEE were established far too late to be effective. However, it gave the populace an excellent if rather extraordinary day out.

According to Tim Stokes

> On St George's Day one hundred years ago, King George V stepped on to the turf of the newly created Wembley Stadium to open the British Empire Exhibition – and in doing so became the first UK royal to make a live radio broadcast.

> Running for two six-month long seasons, in 1924 and 1925, the event saw grand pavilions, life-sized butter sculptures, a coalmine, a recreation of Tutankhamen's tomb and elaborate theatrical performances featuring thousands of people and animals come to a corner of north-west London. (2024)

The idea was to produce a guided tour of Empire so that visitors could see nominal attractions from many countries. In that respect it resembled an old-fashioned carnival, with marching bands and sideshows. It was also intended to encourage trade and, according to Stokes,

> the dominions like Canada and Australia hoped to attract people from the UK to move abroad, while at the same time many were worried about the number of single women who were living in Britain, as a result of how many men died in World War One.
>
> There were also regular performances of the grand-sounding Pageant of Empire, which had a cast of about 15,000 amateur performers along with some 300 horses, 500 donkeys, seven elephants, llamas, bulls, 730 camels, 72 monkeys, three bears, 1000 doves, hawks and a macaw. (2024)

The BEE was designed to raise the hopes of a population who had only very recently come through the horrors of the First World War, where families had been decimated only to be followed by the equally destructive Spanish influenza epidemic. The plan was to entertain people rather than simply lecture them. And yet it made a loss of £1.5m then/£75m now, while the Great Exhibition of 1851 was far more successful financially and better placed in time and location. And therein lies the rub. By 1924, the British Empire was on the wane, and what people came to see was more a highly theatrical demonstration of our past than particularly relevant to 1924.

> In the Canadian pavilion, a working model of Niagara Falls stood near a life sized butter sculpture of the Prince of Wales, with his horse in a huge refrigerated unit…
>
> As for Australia, it displayed sheep-shearing and its own butter sculpture, of legendary England cricketer, Jack Hobbs being bowled… While it may have seemed odd to come face to face with sporting and actual royalty in dairy form, such displays had a very real purpose.
>
> "There's this very romantic ideal that everything can be procured in the empire," says Neal Shasore, head of the London School of

Architecture. "Wembley is a big argument. It's a big physical argument for imperial preference." (Stokes, 2024)

Yet somehow I remain unconvinced. There were other displays dedicated to most of the different territories, designed to show what life was like in different parts of the globe.

> More controversial was the use of nearly 300 non-white colonial people who travelled from across the empire to depict places like Nigeria by living and working in the pavilions. Called "races in residence", such exhibits had been common at similar events previously, and while organisers tried to modernise the idea by shifting the emphasis to education over entertainment, the use of people in displays led to anti-colonialism protest by black London students. (2024)

The term "races in residence" has the feel of something inferior, a hangover from old colonial days. Would the English or the Welsh be described as "races in residence"? I think not, and there is something temporary about the term that precludes ownership. In short, it is patronising. Overall, we should keep in mind that the vast majority of the population did not travel abroad the way we do now. So part of the appeal of the exhibits would have been a sense of strangeness to many members of the audience, but perhaps not so strange as seeing them at a damp Wembley rather than in their own countries.

Parts of it had something of the funfair, particularly the little railway on which the king and queen were filmed; this may have had something to do with why the BEE did not remain long in the memory and why, when John Betjeman toured the site in *Metro-land* nearly 50 years later, there was an air of melancholy about the damp, abandoned buildings, some of which were then used for storage. He thought the pleasure park was one of the best things about it. The fair had moved on and, let's face it, there was nothing very exotic about Wembley Park, then or now. Many of the items that formed part of the exhibition were dispersed to museums all over the world, but even they lacked the exoticism of, say, the Elgin Marbles or a painting by Monet. They were essentially props, that now seem as out of place as the soggy palm trees at Pinewood Studios from when they tried to film *Cleopatra* there in 1962 and were forced to up sticks and decamp to Italy by the good old British weather. This is England, mate, and it just never stops raining.

After its demolition in 1973, two of the Wembley sculptured lions that guarded the British Government pavilion were moved to the Animal Kingdom at Woburn Abbey in Bedfordshire. Betjeman's film thus became the last opportunity to see them intact.

So the hordes who visited this last hurrah of Empire were a captive audience, and many of them used the Met to get there, thus ensuring that they were already on the first rung of the ladder to see what was on offer further up the line. If the Exhibition itself, despite being rubber stamped by the king, was perhaps evidence that the Empire was in decline, as it had been since early in the century, at least the Met was busy building its own little empire in Little England for those who wanted to be part of the new housing boom. The rewards were not necessarily financial but rather offered a position in a smart part of outer suburbia away from the smoke.

But the disastrous Wembley tower, to be at the centre of Wembley Stadium, was a false start, conceived on Met land by the usually surefooted Edward Watkin. The tower had been conceived to compare favourably with others around the globe, the nearest being the Eiffel Tower in Paris. Unfortunately, although it was put out to tender to various well-known architects, only the base was ever constructed when the anticipated interest from the public never materialised; what might have been an emblem to the growth of Metro-land was eventually taken apart. Despite its failures on behalf of Empire, vaulting ambition at least eventually turned part of the Wembley Park Estate into an immensely popular stadium.

So no harm was done to Metro-land – quite the reverse – and I think we can regard Wembley Park, then far less congested, as the southernmost tip of Metro-land, a place not found on any map and nearest in approach to something created by Ealing Studios. There were no passports or entry fees, just the promise of Churchillian "sunlit uplands" that were bound to improve your life. We may look back on this concept and scoff, but how is the dangerous, overtaxed and overburdened populace a quarter of the way through the 21st century any better off? In what we may regard as a simpler age, the positive nature of Metro-land was a blessing when set against the horrors of the First World War and the Spanish flu pandemic. The air in Metro-land was supposedly purer and healthier compared to the bomb sites and slums of London. It may have been a simple aspiration but it was a good one in every sense of the word. And that is what is missing from today. There is no positivity.

So why did Metro-land succeed when the BEE ultimately failed? The answer lies in the much more modest appropriateness of its concept, tailored to a workable idea of the then-modern working man and where he should live. If some of the fluff used to advertise it seemed to drum up country life as it had been a couple of centuries earlier, it was at least recognisably England and not a butter sculpture that would melt away to nothing. The BEE, though it was not intended as such, was more a celebration of the past than a fanfare for the future.

The other major event that helped inspire the Met was the 1948 London Olympic Games, which took place between 29 July and 14 August. This of course was only shortly after the war, when the country was struggling to get back on its feet and ration books were still commonplace. Mindy Johnston advises that

> Despite limited preparation time and after much debate over the need for a sports festival at a time when many countries were still recovering from the destruction of World War II, the 1948 Olympics ultimately were very popular and were perceived as providing relief from the strains caused by the war. (Britannica, 2025)

Of course it was a relatively modest affair, and it was nothing like on the scale of modern Olympic presentations. The emphasis was where it should be: on the sport. But there were certain exceptions, where old wounds had not had a chance to heal.

Germany and Japan, the defeated powers, were not invited to participate. The Soviet Union also did not participate, but fellow communist countries including Hungary, Yugoslavia and Poland did so. The London Games lacked the state-of-the-art facilities that had been used in Los Angeles and Berlin, but the British capital's sports facilities had survived the war in good condition and were adequate for Olympic competition. Wembley Stadium hosted the opening ceremonies, track-and-field and other events. There was no Olympic Village; the male athletes were housed at an army camp in Uxbridge, while the women stayed in dormitories at Southlands College (2025).

There were about 4,000 athletes in total, pretty impressive under the circumstances. However, in true English style, poor weather created problems for the track-and-field competitions, resulting in very few Olympic records.

The women's competition was expanded to ten events with the addition of the 200-metre run, the long jump and the shot put. Fanny

Blankers-Koen, a 30-year-old mother of two, won four gold medals for the Netherlands. Emil Zátopek of Czechoslovakia won the 10,000-metre run, the first of four gold medals in his career. American Bob Mathias became the youngest gold medallist in the decathlon, at age 17 (2025).

The Americans, led by Sammy Lee, won every men's swimming and diving event. Victoria Draves of the United States earned a gold medal in both platform and springboard diving (2025).

Among the Olympic newcomers, László Papp of Hungary won a medal for boxing; Paul Elvstrom of Denmark for yachting and Gert Fredriksson of Sweden won two medals for kayaking. As you might have observed, the British were not obviously represented.

However, the Games were a substantial success given the difficulties of the time, and despite the initial doubts they became a way of encouraging the populace to look forward rather than dwell on the grim past of the two world wars. It was also a tremendous fillip for the Met, with the resulting huge increase in passengers; and, of course, Wembley Stadium has provided regular boosts because of important events like the annual FA Cup Final.

The Metro-land guide painted a gloriously antique picture of the area, assisted by archaic prose that would have seemed well out of date even then.

> the Roman road aslant the eastern border… the innumerable field-paths which mark the labourer's daily route from hamlet to farm. (1932)

Indeed, this quasi-verse form would not have looked out of place in *Hamlet*. It was a ridiculous throwback to the Middle Ages, written by someone who had perhaps rather too much of the local brew while composing it. No doubt he spent the rest of the sunlit afternoon asleep on a haystack.

However, not everyone saw it that way. Five years before the Second World War, composer Constant Lambert offered a more cynical view, stating that the area

> conjure[d] up the hideous faux bonhomie of the hiker, noisily wading his way through the petrol pumps of Metroland, singing obsolete sea chanties [*sic*] with the aid of the Week-End Book, imbibing

chemically-flavoured synthetic beer under the impression that he is tossing off a tankard of "jolly good ale and old". (1934)

More recently Christian Wolmar, a historian of the London Underground, saw the advertising of the time as suggesting

> the world of Metroland is not cluttered with people, the suburban streets are empty… There are it seems, more farm animals than people. (2004)

Of course, the advertising trade has never been known for its attention to detail and scrupulous honesty, and the flowery style of writing in promoting Metro-land was only a more extreme version of the exotic posters used to promote the Great Western Railway, where the towns en route were crime-free havens of joy and sunshine that might have been dreamed up by Enid Blyton. So Metro-land was envisaged as an unspoilt topography, entirely free of threat, the sins of the past expunged. Had the Pilgrim Fathers, many years earlier, been aware of it, they might have abandoned the discomforts of an Atlantic sea voyage and settled rather closer to home, north-west of London.

Another view was offered by the reliably cynical A. N. Wilson. In *After the Victorians* he observed that

> as [the husband] went off to the nearest station every morning… the wife, half liberated and half slave, stayed behind wondering how many of the newly invented domestic appliances they could afford to purchase, and how long the man would hold on to his job in the Slump. No wonder when the war came, that so many of these suburban prisoners felt a sense of release. (2005)

Rather overdone perhaps since this seems to rule out the possibility of the wife being capable of individual thought, which almost places Wilson in the same category as that aspect of Metro-land that he is criticising. At the time women may have regarded their homes as a new freedom, a release from being told what to do by the government. Also, I cannot believe that the outbreak of war could ever have been regarded as a "release". But he is correct in describing the semi-detached properties of the new suburbia as "pokey", despite their claims of individuality, toy-soldier versions of the larger Tudorbethan properties of the stockbroker belt of Middlesex and Surrey. Yes, there was a sense of uniformity but at the time it was seen, quite reasonably, as a step up from the bombed-out chaos of wartime.

Also, in our hierarchy of needs, we are not so very different from one another. It is more a question of ambition and levels and a desire to escape the stuffy shackles of Victorian England. Whereas the factory estates offered by the Victorian entrepreneurs were built to make it easier for the labourers both to get to work and put in their best efforts once they got there, Metro-land's homes offered a solace from the daily grind. The only string was that they used the railway to get to work, thus subtly enabling the Met to expand. While the loyal company man who spends his entire working life with one firm may be a thing of the past, many people like to belong, either explicitly or implicitly. So A. N. Wilson, while amusing in his caustic remarks, may simply have misread human nature. Our identity is determined by how we fit in with others. In isolation we are nothing. Only the great explorers are capable of dealing with that.

After the Second World War some architects derided suburbia as uninspiring, suggesting that each estate was interchangeable with any other, wherever it was in the country. There is, of course, some truth in that, the underlying idea being that it did not bring out the best in the post-war Englishman in terms of ambition, and suggested a life ruled by monotony. Most governments in recent times, however, have enjoyed subverting their populace to hard work while steadily removing part of what they earn through ever-increasing taxes. There is a limit to how far you can go along that road without it becoming counter productive, instead creating disaffection and a new breed of poor who are forced to choose between heating and eating long before they think about earning money. At the same time it throws more people onto the benefits scrapheap. But at the time of Metro-land this level of negativity was absent, and the newly suburbanised owners were hopeful of an upward trajectory to their lives. We seem to have entirely lost that sense of vision of the Victorian age and after, driven by entrepreneurs of a different class. Without the dynamism of such people as Edward Watkin, we are left in a country where not only Empire has disappeared but even the old country itself. Given our great and ancient cathedrals, designed and built without modern assistance, what sort of depths have we sunk to that the end of the millennium can only be celebrated with something as trite as the O2 Arena, and only talentless pop idols, so-called influencers and film stars, passing phenomena, are held up as something worth aspiring to?

Our politicians, totally devoid of vision, seem more than ever to lack direction, while the state, ostensibly a force for good, is now regarded as both an omnipotent and yet incompetent oracle, supposedly superior to the private sector but actually failing in most crucial respects. The public sector is like a macro version of the NHS, drowning in a sea of incompetent managers while the nurses and doctors at the coal face, many of whom are exceptional, struggle to keep up. Our values have thus become twisted, and nothing in this country seems to work properly. Free speech is now banned and any criticism immediately dubbed racist or misogynistic. Hate crimes are rife and the thought police of Orwell's vision are now here to try and subvert us while real crime – burglary, GBH and murder – go improperly investigated while the police prefer to bend the knee to every newly fashionable cause. Rainbow's end.

ONWARDS AND OUTWARDS

When completed, the Met Line was of considerable length, running during rush hour all the way from Aldgate to either Uxbridge, Watford, Amersham or Chesham, although the latter was originally served off peak by a push and pull to Chalfont and Latimer. Also, off peak, the line terminated at Baker Street, giving passengers a choice of other underground lines, the Circle Line in particular. It was only a five-minute walk from Marylebone mainline station and the Chiltern Line, which ran alongside the Met for much of its length.

The Metropolitan is scarcely an underground line at all; its trains are larger (like the Circle) and it is only underground in London, emerging, blinking into the daylight, at Finchley Road. Whenever I arrive at Finchley Road, I wonder how the buildings, stacked high at the start of the tunnel, could possibly be adequately supported. But they have remained safe for many years. After that, the Metropolitan becomes distinctly overground, in line with its imagined superiority, as it bypasses tube stations such as Kilburn and Dollis Hill. During rush hour some of the Metropolitan trains run fast from Finchley Road to Harrow-on-the-Hill, missing out Wembley Park and the smaller conurbations of Preston Road and Northwick Park. These trains were not really built for speed and it could be quite an uncomfortable journey, particularly if you were seated at the end of a carriage, over the bogey. There was much swaying of the coaches, particularly when negotiating a set of points, and trying to walk about within the coach was sometimes problematic.

Harrow takes its name from Harrow Hill, some 408ft in height, which is to be found about half a mile south of the town. Despite its apparent modernity, the original village dates back to medieval times. The 11th-century church of St Mary's gives witness to that. The Anglo-Saxon Chronicles record Harrow Hill in 767 as *Gumeninga Hergae*, which may mean the heathen temple of a long-forgotten tribe called the Gumeningas, or sons of Gumenga. Later, in 1398, there is a reference to *Harrowe atte Hille*, a place of pagan worship. However, we should not get too concerned by this, as pagan simply means a country dweller holding non-mainstream religious views, not necessarily a worshipper of evil. Harrow was an ancient parish in the Gore Hundred of Middlesex, which covered a large rural area taking in Pinner, Harrow Weald, Wealdstone and, believe it or not, Wembley. I am grateful to Wikipedia 2025 for the above information. What this piece of local history reminds us of is the long-forgotten fact that England was once ruled and controlled in terms of relatively small tribal kingdoms, rather than a central authoritative hub.

When the Met's new railway station opened in Harrow in 1880, the modern town that we know today grew up around it. The original village was located a little distance away, on the hill itself. Perhaps the most significant historical point is that Charles I, on his way to surrender to the Scottish Army, took a tea break at Harrow Hill for a final glimpse of London before everything went horribly wrong with the temporary dislocation of monarchical tradition. Indeed, a commemorative plaque exists on Grove Hill, where the nearby spring is referred to as King Charles' Well.

Harrow became a London borough in 1965, having been transferred from Middlesex. In a sense, that marks the inevitable march of Greater London towards the outer suburbs, and the Met must take its share of the blame for that. But, for me, Harrow has always seemed rather an unapproachable town; just too big, too commercial and therefore unappealing. The railway station has, after all, six platforms: four for the Met and two for the Chiltern Line, sometimes shared by the Met. From the Met's point of view, it was undoubtedly a success; all those new homes feeding in to the railway. The problem is that now much of the town seems soulless, which I think rather defeats the idea that the elders of Metro-land had in mind: practical yet a touch romantic and aware of its past. The history of the town has been largely buried in favour of a thick layer of commercialism.

Harrow School is a significant boarding public school for boys and has a long history, founded nearly five hundred years ago in 1572 by wealthy farmer John Lyon; the school was set up under a royal charter granted by Elizabeth I. There is a strong sense of superiority about it, especially since the uniform included morning suits, straw boaters and canes. John Betjeman covers it briefly in 1973's *Metro-land*. Whether this attitude still has a place in Starmer's England remains to be seen but, as we know, he is doing his best to destroy it. Yet the school's official name is "The Free Grammar School of John Lyon within the town of Harrow-on-the-Hill". According to Wikipedia (2025), "there is some evidence of a grammar school at Harrow in the mid-16th century". Whether this indicates that the original was not as posh as it subsequently became is not entirely clear, but we do know that John Lyon's school was founded to provide a free education for 30 (later extended to 40) poor boys of the parish. However, the School Master was permitted to accept "foreigners" (boys from outside the parish) from whom he received fees. It was the need for foreigners to find accommodation that led to the concept of boarding. As in all schools of the time, education was based on the languages and culture of the ancient civilisations of Rome and Greece (2025).

At the time of the school's foundation, the Catholic Church had only recently been cast from favour by Henry VIII with the dissolution of the monasteries, but the idea of teaching from Latin and Greek origins lingered on. From this we can deduce that Harrow School's education system was extremely high minded, despite its original intention of assisting the less fortunate of the parish.

According to Wikipedia

> The founder John Lyon died in 1592, bequeathing his estate to two beneficiaries: the school and [strangely] the maintenance of two roads, the Harrow Road and the Edgware Road, both going to London, 10 miles (16km) away. The road trust received by far the greater share, the school's share providing just for the salary of The School Master and some minor provisions.
>
> This situation, reasonable at the time because of the need to transport merchandise to market, continued until 1991 when the considerable assets of the Road Trust were reassigned to John Lyon's Charity, a charity to provide educational benefits for the inhabitants of the boroughs through which the roads pass. It was only after the death of Lyon's wife in 1608 that the construction of the school building began. Known as the Old Schools, it was completed in 1615. (2025)

Much of the Old Schools remains. An extension was carried out by Charles Robert Cockerell in 1818 and the building, including its redesign, is now Grade I listed. Harrow School is a bastion of Metro-land and just one of the many buildings of interest that make up this area.

The number of pupils eventually rose to over 800, but until relatively recently in its long history, the school had (as did many public schools of that time) a system of fagging, in which the freshers had to undertake menial tasks in their first year, including serving the more senior boys.

The idea was to instil in the younger boys the belief that they could not "rule" effectively unless they had also experienced the concept of servitude.

I was one of the last intake to public schools to understand what that was like. I remember, at the age of 13, staring depressedly into a hugely stained milk saucepan that had been used by the housemaster and prefects and wondering how I was ever going to get it clean. When I eventually became a prefect myself and was in turn supplied with a fag, I couldn't think of anything much for him to do as I always preferred to look after myself. Looking back on it now, it strikes me as a very Dickensian and humiliating system that, even then, seemed to belong to a previous century. But then I never quite subscribed to the rather arrogant view that the pupils of a boys' public school had the inbuilt right to lord it over others, either at school or afterwards in life. An informal photograph taken in my latter years there appears to show an arrogance in the curious positioning of the boys taking part, each in a strange but somehow superior pose. I like to think that that attitude has mostly died out, but consequently, I am inclined to the view that the conceivers of Metro-land intended it for everyone rather than just the privileged few, even though its directors were often from a privileged class.

The other common aspect of public schools at that time was the concept of beating boys for what were usually very minor infringements and, where I was, a list was posted outside the headmaster's door every day. It seemed to me strange that there was always a regular number of misdeeds waiting to be punished, come rain or shine. Later on I realised that the man was a sadist who took pleasure in what he did and had no business being a monk. This kind of cruelty should not have been inflicted and harked back to earlier times when impromptu punishments out of all proportion to the crime were dished out to the populace without any investigation as to justification. Just as females were badly treated by the courts, with sanctimonious judgements handed out often based on their sex rather than the background to the crime, so the boys at English public schools were wrongly targeted by those who should never have been teachers in the first place. When I met this man in later life, now no longer in proper control of himself and dribbling down his soiled habit for others to clean up, I didn't feel pity, only a sense of him getting what he deserved.

And yet that public school privilege can go hopelessly wrong. There was a contemporary of mine at public school who I always envied as he seemed to me to encapsulate everything that was needed for school and in life afterwards. He was as excellent at sport, then a must at my school, as he was at academic work. Harry seemed set for a life of great success. Yet he was also kind and considerate so we got on well. I lost touch with him after leaving school until one day I received a letter from my ex-housemaster telling me that Harry had somehow been taken into the grip of the Moonies, a cult that held considerable sway at that time. How had he made such a mistake? Worse still, in an effort to escape their clutches he had jumped out of a window and injured himself badly, ending up in a wheelchair. I immediately offered to visit him but, before I could do so, I heard that he had passed away; a sad reflection of the young man who had everything to live for and had somehow come to grief. There is, of course, a large part of this tale which I will never know, but it gave me pause to think that going to a public school is no absolute guarantee of a comfortable life. Some public-school boys end up in prison and I remember one, set on making shedloads of money very fast by less than totally transparent means, was definitely headed in the wrong direction. I nearly fell for this scam but luckily came to my senses in good time.

However, there is no doubting Harrow School's history and famous alumni. These include a number of former prime ministers including Peel, Palmerston, Baldwin and Churchill. The Indian prime minister Nehru (who we should not mention in connection with Edwina Mountbatten) also attended as well as members of both Houses of Parliament, various royal families, three Nobel Prize winners and no less than 20 Victoria Cross holders. It also boasts many other significant alumni in both the arts and sciences.

Many public schools lost their almost automatic feeder prep schools through circumstances beyond their control. Parents were no longer convinced to send their offspring through the usual routes and, particularly with regard to Catholic schools, there was no longer a conviction that they must attend a Catholic prep school. This came about through both cost and a gradual weakening of the ethos of a Christian society. The public schools dealt with this in different ways, either by taking in girls and becoming co-educational or buying up a prep school so that the feed was still there. Merchant Taylors' is a good example of that. Whether the public schools will survive the VAT raid on their fees remains to be seen. However, it seems likely that those that remain will only be there for the very wealthy. After all, the term public school is, at any rate, something of a misnomer. Unfortunately, at the time of writing, there is no longer any effective opposition in Parliament, the Conservatives having blown a substantial majority by disappearing up their own fundament.

At Harrow, the line splits, where some trains undertake a branch to Rayners Lane and Uxbridge, but somehow I always considered this something of an irrelevance, not really a key part of the Metropolitan Line and, indeed, it took a long while for it to become a properly established branch. Harrow is a key entry point to Metro-land because it was there that the garden estates that make up quintessential Met suburbia are to be found, being mostly constructed in the 1920s and 1930s. At first glance they may appear run of the mill, but each property, even if not very large, contains small differences from its neighbour in such things as window or door design, with small stained-glass motifs and such like. They were set well back from the tree-lined avenue, behind a hedge or wall, beyond which was a pavement and a verge before you reached the road. So whereas the countryside had been dug up to facilitate these villas, they were not so unpleasant providing you did not set the bar too high. And, at the time, most of the incumbents would not have had the means for anything more spacious, such as those found in Hertfordshire and Buckinghhamshire. In order to understand them we need to step back one hundred years to understand the post-war aspirations of these new residents. There wasn't the money around there is now and many a man might spend his entire working life with one company. But as we know to our cost, company loyalty is no longer rewarded and employees find themselves dismissed by text message, with little concern for their future. Allegedly, it is all about the bottom line or, rather more likely, the pockets of the directors and shareholders. How times have changed! Dog eat dog.

One of the joys of Harrow, or rather Harrow Weald, is the splendid edifice of Grim's Dyke, much beloved of the late Poet Laureate, John Betjeman. It was built in the 19th century, by the architect Richard Norman Shaw, in the Gothic style for the painter Frederick Goodall. Betjeman saw it as a forerunner of modern housing, but there I cannot quite agree. It is too heavy, too individual and, one might also add, rather pompous though not without interest. What is rather more enlightening, according to Harry Turner, is the land's history, which harks back to the first century.

> It was at this time that the land was not known as Grim's Dyke but rather "Grim's Ditch" – a name which refers to the Iron Age earthworks

that can be found across southern England. Dated to the fifth and sixth centuries, if not even further back, the earthwork consists of a v-shaped ditch that has visible remains stretching from Pinner Green to Harrow Weald Common – a swathe of land on which the estate at Old Redding was eventually built. This ditch is believed to be a defensive structure built by the Catuvellauni tribe to aid in the ongoing struggle at the time with the Roman forces in the region.

As one of the most powerful Celtic tribes in southern Britain, with territory extending as far as the northern bank of the Thames to what is modern-day Hertfordshire, the Catuvellauni were leaders of the opposition to the Roman invasion until their eventual defeat and subjugation in the early first century. Grim's Dyke remains one of the few remaining monuments to this prehistoric struggle. (2025)

It seems strange that if we go sufficiently far back in history, England was made up, as were so many European countries, of small kingdoms of very territorial tribes, intent not only on keeping what they had but also extending their reach. The Catuvellauni were just one of those, but unfortunately they proved no match for the invading Romans who, whilst they may have set up camp in England, never bothered with what they regarded as the more savage Ireland.

In 1890, William Schwenck Gilbert, one half of the Savoy Operas duo, purchased the Grim's Dyke for £4,000 and both lived and farmed on the estate with his wife Lucy. They had a number of exotic pets and, according to Harry Turner (2016), these included a couple of ring-tailed lemurs from Madagascar called Adam and Eve. Eventually these two produced a third lemur, named Paul, although that somehow seems a misnomer.

Gilbert was known for his kindness but he could also be rather prickly. There is also a story, although it may be apocryphal, that the owner of the adjoining estate, a famous jam maker, one day accused Gilbert of trespassing. Gilbert replied: "Far be it from me to tread on your preserves…"

But while Grim's Dyke was his life, it also became responsible for his death when he was giving swimming lessons to a couple of local girls, Ruby Preece and Winifred Emery, in a lake on the estate. One of them got into difficulties and, in trying to rescue her, Gilbert suffered a massive heart attack and died due to the physical exertion. As a result, Lady Gilbert had the lake drained; eventually it silted up, but not without producing several smaller ponds where, in 2011, the rare greater crested newt was found. Gilbert, had he lived, would have been delighted.

The push to extend the Met Line in the ten years following 1880 was remarkable, with Pinner reached in 1885, Rickmansworth in 1887 and Chesham in 1889. A contemporary account claims that

> The extension of the Metropolitan Railway… has opened up a new and delightful countryside to the advantage of picturesque seekers, ancient houses and old-world ways. Within 50 minutes from Baker Street and for the cost of less than a florin (10p), if the visitor be economically disposed, he can enjoy a feast of good things, fresh air, noble parks, stately houses, magnificent trees and sylvan streams. (18, 1986)

The attempts in contemporary literature to depict an idyllic countryside were common at the time. However, there was some opposition.

> A reader of the *Financial News* complained that "so boring was the country passed through and so few people on the train" that he considered that the extension "was a waste of money and doomed to failure". (18, 1986)

But then the line was never about what you could see from the windows and yet, while the line became a great success, one would have to agree that the countryside between Harrow and, say, Northwood as well as out to Uxbridge is rather bland; the ribbon development and generally flat topography do not have much to offer. It is not until you get as far as Moor Park that this changes to something more interesting.

So let's now take a look at Pinner, a town with rather more obvious history and appeal than some of the other stops on the line, both before and after it, even if these days it is considered a part of the rapidly expanded Harrow. I am grateful to Harrowonline (2024) for much of the following information about Pinner, which has its own annual fair that goes back in history and was also celebrated by John Betjeman in *Metro-land* (1973). The town is about 12 miles north-west of London, far enough away to be separate from it and to have one of the lowest crime rates in the Greater London area. It has managed, more than most, to hold on to its links with the past. We cannot count the fact that someone drove into the back of my car in Pinner as a crime, though it seemed like it at the time. I also frequented a dentist with gold-rimmed glasses on the outskirts of Pinner, a Mr Entwhistle, a visitor from the north, and the temptation to refer to him as Dentwhistle often proved rather too much to resist. When I damaged my teeth very badly in an accident, his hand shook and he was unable to cope, dispatching me instead to Wimpole Street for treatment, and I never saw him again. But I digress.

The history of Pinner probably goes back a thousand years with the first record of *Pinnora* appearing in 1231. Of course, the name of the town derives from the proximity of the River (it hardly merits the name) Pinn which snakes through the town. The sloping high street is rather attractive with some older buildings to give it character. It is here that the annual fair is held.

The oldest part of the town is that close to St John the Baptist's church, which dates from the 14th century. The name goes back even earlier to 1234, when it existed as a Chapel of Ease to St Mary's in Harrow. After that it was then rebuilt and indeed re-dedicated in 1321. This meant that it became entirely separate and independent of St Mary's in 1766, after a hiatus of nearly 450 years. The first vicar was apparently not appointed until 1868 so one assumes the church was still reliant on an arrangement for a cleric from elsewhere in the interim. Harrowonline tells us that

> It [Pinner] was initially inhabited by yeoman farmers, small holders and labourers, and was the largest settlement in the Manor of Harrow, as it used to be known when the Lord of the Manor was none other than the Archbishop of Canterbury. (2024)

It is worth making the point that both before and after the dissolution of the monasteries, the Church, be it initially Catholic and thereafter Protestant, had a tremendous influence on the life and control of the populace. Well into the 20th century, the local cleric was often ensconced in a grand house and was at least as much a local squire and landowner as he was a man of the cloth. Therefore, the founding of what were originally small outposts along the line often have as much to do with clerical influence as political. It was only in the second half of the 20th century that the grip of the Church loosened and the people largely turned their back on it in favour of more commercial interests. As the product of a monastic upbringing, I can affirm the weakening effects of that even in my lifetime. The dwindling population of Benedictine monks at Downside were recently shipped off to join the community at Buckfast Abbey (otherwise known as Fast Buck due to its commercial instincts) following a series of scandals that, while it only involved a very few of the monks, rendered the remainder, whose script for managing a modern public school was woefully out of touch, no longer fit for purpose. Since then I have heard that the ageing population of under a dozen are now to be shipped to Belmont in Herefordshire. It was all announced with a fanfare but actually it is more a dissolution of the remaining monks. While this difficulty by no means concerned just Downside – a number of schools both Catholic and otherwise were affected – it seemed to hasten the end of the era of clerical influence. In addition, the very recent addition of VAT to private-school fees was just another Labour-driven nail in its determination to remove privilege from the agenda, except of course for its own hierarchy where it became somehow strangely acceptable: clothing, spectacles, free concert tickets and all.

In harness with that clerical control, there was also that of the local landowners, who had both the money and their own interests in developing a railway to serve their local purposes.

> Towards the end of the 18th century, a daily coach to London was established, thus strengthening its travel links with the city and making it more popular for people to come and live in Pinner. In 1837, the London and Birmingham Railway cut across the north-east corner of Pinner, and – in 1842 – a railway station (now Hatch End station) opened. (2024)

Of course the odd folly was built, sometimes in a line of otherwise ordinary houses. I remember being fascinated by once such in Hatch End, with all sorts of odd shapes to the building and different-coloured bricks. It hung around for a while before the council got nervous and, disapproving, razed this individuality to the ground. To live in Metroland, there had to be some sense of compliance within its ethos. Go too far and you would be flung out on your ear. They may not have realised it but the good citizens of the then new builds in Harrow were doing just that: complying. In doing so they were fulfilling the plans of the Metropolitan Railway and became, as it were, Metropolitan Man. Even my family, stuck out as far as Northwood, were unknowingly fitting in with it, and where the female of the species had yet to make her mark beyond the confines of genteel cocktail parties of a Sunday morning.

Pinner was originally yet another agricultural area and there is a certain irony between the language of the Met leaflets, with its emphasis on pastoral rurality, and the fact that the builders of the line were actually systematically destroying that countryside as it pushed further out towards Buckinghamshire.

> By the time the Metropolitan Railway reached Pinner (in 1885), one can safely say that Pinner was no longer purely an agricultural area, as it initially was. Rayners Lane station [named after a farmer Rayner] opened in 1904, with North Harrow station to follow in 1915. (2024)

Rayner must have been quite an influential man, such that the station, rather than taking its name from the area or local highways, selected him.

While neither of these were major stops along the Met's route, their presence was enough to spur rows of ribbon development along the route, eventually spreading outwards and away from the line. While neither Pinner nor North Harrow can be regarded as particularly significant or, perish the thought, holiday/weekend destinations, they were just more dots on the proposed route map that the Met was determined to join up.

However, Pinner, more than most, has managed to retain some sense of identity, and the garden estates were developed. The Pinner Wood estate conservation area grew round the centre of the town and contains a number of art deco homes which were constructed nearly a hundred years ago. Elm Park Court has a Grade II listing. There are also a number of green spaces, including the Pinner Memorial Park, Pinner Village Gardens and Pinner Wood.

As already mentioned, Pinner's annual fair was originally granted by Royal Charter, making it one of the oldest in the country (1336). In this way, a sense of community has been maintained.

> Celebrations include the "Ye Olde Wheelbarrow Race", an event unique to Pinner, in which a team of two take turns to push their respective partners around Pinner while drinking beer. (2024)

Most trains continued on to Rickmansworth and Watford. In those days the line beyond Rickmansworth was not electrified, which caused complications for those trains bound for the Chilterns. How this was overcome is explained later in the book.

So after Moor Park and before Rickmansworth, there was a steep right branch towards Croxley and Watford, entering a short tunnel as it did so. You could also take advantage of it from the Rickmansworth end. A plan to connect this to Watford Junction on the London/

Midland line never came to anything, and the Metropolitan's final stop at Watford was a substantial distance from the centre due to concerns about the line defiling Cassiobury Park. John Betjeman celebrates the Croxley Green revels in his 1973 film *Metro-land*. A young queen of the revels was appointed every year and though her powers were extremely limited, it harked back to a time of parochialism in England, when the populations of different areas were not remotely connected to each other and relied on messengers to promulgate the news to individual parishes.

Rickmansworth never really figured as a significant place in my childhood. It was simply a station to be gone through on the way to somewhere else, even though originally there was more than one railway. In the days of steam that ended in the 1960s, it was the end of the electrified line from London and, consequently, where the electric locomotive on onward-bound Chiltern trains had to be swapped for a tank engine to take the carriages for the rest of the journey. I may not have done the town justice but it seems now to be over developed.

Seventeen miles out of London and five miles away from Watford, Rickmansworth is now just another dormitory town on the M25 and inside its perimeter. Wikipedia tells us that

> Rickmansworth is the administrative seat of the Three Rivers District Council; the confluence of the River Chess and the River Gade with the Colne in Rickmansworth inspired the district's name. The enlarged Colne flows south to form a major tributary of the River Thames.
>
> The name Rickmansworth derives from the Saxon name *Ryckmer*, the local landowner, and *worth* meaning a farm or stockade. (2025)

There were countless other spellings over the years, the most outlandish of which comes from the Domesday Book in 1086 where it is referred to as the manor of Prichemaresworde.

According to Wikipedia

> There was a settlement in this part of the Colne Valley in the Stone Age. Rickmansworth was one of five manors with which the great Abbey of St Albans had been endowed when founded in 793 by King Offa of Mercia. Local tithes supported the abbey, which provided the clergy until the dissolution of the monasteries in 1539. Around the time of the Domesday Book, the population of "Prichmareworth" may have been about 200. (2025)

> From the above we can see the amount of control the early church had over the population. We should not be concerned about the various differences in spelling at that time. It was commonplace until Caxton (with his printing press) and Chaucer introduced a degree of standardisation. Before that there was not even any set convention as to the construction of a sentence, let alone spelling.
>
> So it was that Cardinal Wolsey, as Abbot of St Albans, was overall responsible. It should also be remembered that the parish of Rickmansworth encompassed a much wider area than simply what is now the town. It took in Batchworth, Chorleywood, Croxley Green, Mill End and West Hyde, albeit with a much smaller population.
>
> In 1851, the population had grown to 4,800, and the parish was divided. St Mary's Church serves the parish concentrated in the town and extending to Batchworth and parts of Moor Park. The town had a population of 14,571 recorded at the 2001 census. (2025)

Since then it has continued to grow considerably.

> The three rivers, the Colne, Chess and Gade, provided water for the watercress trade and power for corn milling, silk weaving, paper making and brewing, all long gone. Other industries have included leather-tanning, soft drinks, laundry, straw-plaiting and stocking production. Now the rivers, canal and gravel pits provide for recreation. (2025)

Despite the coming of the railway, it was Watford that grew at a greater rate, having a negative effect on some of the local industries; possibly because it was situated on the main line.

From Rickmansworth – and, as a child, I always wondered how they managed to get such a long name on the front of a train – the line climbs steeply towards the Chilterns, leaving the last remnants of suburbia behind it. Arriving at Chorleywood, one of the least used stations on the Met, I often wondered at the reasons for this. Was it because the population, close to open country and with wealthy houses tucked behind iron gates, had no need of a station or was it simply that the station was inconveniently situated? Chorleywood common provides a splendid piece of countryside dotted with trees, its southern border near the railway. I remember setting out to have a picnic on the common one boiling hot day in 1976 with my wife and her mother, only to find, when we unpacked, that the latter had forgotten to bring anything to drink.

Parched from the unusually hot sun, we crawled towards the nearest pub to sate our thirst. Those long hot summers of my youth seem to encapsulate everything that is best about Metro-land, fulfilling its original vision of idyllic country Sundays as described in the Met's leaflets, even without the necessary liquid refreshment.

THE UXBRIDGE BRANCH

The seven-mile branch from Harrow-on-the-Hill to Uxbridge shares its tracks with the Piccadilly Line. The only station exclusive to the Met is West Harrow and, although you would never have known it, this now totally suburbanised route was once almost entirely countryside when the line was first considered. It leaves Harrow-on-the-Hill by means of a burrowing junction under the Met and Chiltern Lines, similar to the one north of Wembley Park and occupied by what is now the Bakerloo. It travels through West Harrow, Eastcote, West Ruislip and Ruislip Manor, as well as Ickenham and Hillingdon, terminating at Uxbridge. It was once the poor relation of the Met's main line due to poor footfall and could be compared to the Watford branch, where the line was forced to terminate well short of the town centre. Eventually it was a massive building plan that saved the Uxbridge branch while, of course, inevitably obliterating its original rural nature. It's just that unlike the suburbs on the main line, the construction took rather longer to achieve. To me, it has never had quite the same appeal as the main line, the topography of the area being largely bland and flat. But the problem with Greater London has always been that it has never stopped growing; the M25 ring has led to even further growth so that everything within it is now loosely labelled Greater London, when in my youth the M25 was not there and, thus, nor was the feeling of urban enclosure.

Looking back on it, it seems as if the Met was, at times, a little too ambitious in its desire to take over everything in the north-west suburbs. The early situation on the Uxbridge branch seems to confirm that, and it must have been a loss maker, even if things turned out all right ultimately. Horne tells us that

> As was often the case, fund-raising proved difficult and this was not helped by much of the route being very thinly populated. The Metropolitan Railway offered to rescue the scheme [from the District] (having had eyes on Uxbridge itself when promoting an unsuccessful Act in 1881) and an Act of 1899 was passed which authorised a link

from Harrow-on-the-Hill to a junction with the Harrow and Uxbridge where it was crossed by Rayners Lane, then a remote trackway... Met trains to Uxbridge began on 4th July 1904; the only intermediate station along the line (described as "mainly grassland") was at Ruislip, commodious facilities being built there for passengers and goods. (26, 2003)

London Transport tells us that

> You had to stand on the narrow strip of footpath beside muddy Rayners Lane to get your ticket to town in 1930. This hut is typical of many of the Metropolitan halts. Rayners Lane opened in 1906 and was the junction for the District Railway to Ealing and London.
>
> Mr A Joce of Eastcote recalls waiting for a train home in the "rush hour" before the First World War. "The air was filled with the singing of countless larks, and the scent of the hayfields. The only signs of life were the distant barns of Rayners Farm on the way to Pinner."... The first houses at Rayners Lane were built for £895 or so by A Robinson and one of the inducements to visit his estate was a refund on your ticket if you called at the estate office. (56, 1983)

Even here the emphasis on idyllic countryside is present and the "countless larks" (really?) stand in counterpoint to "muddy Rayners Lane". The practicality must have been less appealing.

The rather bleak, windswept fields that made up Eastcote before building began can be summed up by the following.

> All one could see from Eastcote station looking south was about three houses and The Pavilion in the spread of fields and open space. (Edwards & Pilgram, 59, 1986)

From the above we can see that the Met was taking a considerable risk in building a line through what was initially barren fields since there was inevitably a delay in producing a passenger revenue stream until construction, itself a slow process, translated into a working population who would board the train to town. Particularly so on this branch where there was substantially less demand. This, of course, is why there was initially a two-car shuttle service, Harrow to Uxbridge, until such time as a through service was justified. The First World War again slowed up development since all effort went into supporting food supplies, where the Met was ideally placed to contribute on its yet unbuilt land. Even after the war, it was not all utilised.

It may seem surprising that boarding a train at Rayners Lane was such a primitive matter as late as 1930 when the station had been open for nearly 25 years, but the reason for this is simply that the Uxbridge branch didn't have the footfall to justify better conditions until some of the new estates took hold, as hinted at in the above quotation. The station was situated on what was originally Bourne Lane or Pinner Lane but was named after Farmer Rayner, who owned a large farmhouse near the site, which demonstrates the fantastic change from the pastoral scene described in the quotation to the suburbia we know now. There is a certain irony in the fact that whereas the Metro-land leaflets described, in archaic terms, the bucolic countryside near the track, in fact it was the Met which was actually progressively destroying it with its building boom, and pushing that idyllic countryside further and further away from London. One of the first of these estates was Harrow Garden Village, which was built for close access to Rayners Lane station. Without this building it was unlikely that the Met would have been able to maintain this branch, even as a shuttle to Harrow, where it was necessary to change for the London train.

When you alight at Rayners Lane station, one of the first things that takes your eye in an otherwise fairly unremarkable street is the Zoroastrian Centre, an art deco Grade II listed building of some style which was originally the Grosvenor Cinema, then the Ace, and then, back in my day, the Odeon. Originally designed by Frank Bromige in 1936, this is a treat for the eyes which gave its patrons plenty to look at, not just on the screen, but in the decoration inside and out. According to Wikipedia,

> Ace cinema is streamlined Art Deco in style, the façade featuring a central concrete sculpted design of a stylised elephant's head with trunk. The auditorium has a circle that originally seated 405 and stalls that originally seated 830. There was originally a stage 44 feet deep and six dressing rooms, and the oval foyer has a sunken area that contained a café. (2025)

I remember being massively impressed by this building even then, a star amongst the rather dull suburban shops around it.

The cinema first opened in 1936 and the following year it became part of the Odeon chain, although the name was not changed to Odeon until 1941. "Oscar Deutsch Entertains Our Nation": while it sounds German, and therefore unlikely to be popular during the Second World War, Deutsch, the founder of the Odeon chain, then the largest cinema chain in the country, was actually of Hungarian Jewish descent. In 1950 the name changed again to the Gaumont and then, quite correctly I think, back to the Odeon in 1964 with a 5 per cent reduction in seating capacity, presumably to improve comfort levels. The Rank Organisation then wanted to convert it to a bingo hall but that was refused by Harrow Council. Therefore in 1981 it was sold to Ace, a smaller group, and renamed accordingly.

However, it lasted no longer than five years in this form and from 1991 became the Grosvenor Cine/Bar Experience, with the Ace Bar in the foyer and a nightclub in the redesigned auditorium. Unfortunately this was not an Experience anyone seemed to want; it failed to attract the punters and closed a few years later. In 2000 it became the Zoroastrian Centre, a religious faith organisation of Asian origin. And so it has been for the past quarter century. At least the building now has some standing in the community after some ill thought out and failed projects of the past, even if the current name conjures up, quite incorrectly, rather primitive spaceships and aliens to this boy, raised quite properly on the BBC's radio success *Journey Into Space* with, I think, occasional interludes from the svelte and charming David Jacobs amongst a revolving cast.

My own experience of it as a cinema was somewhat ruffled when, during a break in the proceedings, a collecting tin was passed round for the RAF. Whereas I have nothing but praise for the RAF and what it has achieved, I do rather object to having a collection plate passed round when I am in a captive environment and have paid my whack for a seat to watch a film. The same annoyance was felt, even more strongly, when seated at a table in a restaurant and someone came round trying to sell flowers. Simply unacceptable in those circumstances. But I digress again.

Of course matters suffered a major interruption due to the First World War and the pandemic of Spanish "flu" that followed it, both of which decimated the number of able-bodied men. During the war, the Met, ever resourceful, used some of the strips of land they owned to grow vegetables to assist the meagre diet of the railwaymen that worked for them.

Eastcote, further along the line, sported Captain Bayly's "Pavilion" Pleasure Grounds in Field End Road where, allegedly, up to 4,000 people could be accommodated. There the punters could find a donkey derby, swings and various other attractions. It may seem fairly primitive to modern eyes, but the population of Eastcote at the time clearly enjoyed it; we were less sophisticated in those days. I am grateful to London Transport for this information.

While many of the houses were limited to relatively small dwellings designed to make up the new garden estates springing up all over this area, there were some larger and more exclusive dwellings too. In 1933, St Lawrence Drive in Eastcote became the site of some more substantial mock Tudor homes constructed by Comben and Wakeling. This site had been chosen as special because it was once the home of a Bank of England Governor. Yet all was not completely lost, as there were still some woods nearby. The point is that, even in Metro-land, there was still a hierarchy, from drones to directors, and you needed to know your place within it.

Metro-land was, as described in *Modernism in Metro-land*,

> influenced by the Garden Suburb movement and due to its innate Englishness, the default architectural style of Metro-land was nostalgic; a mixture of Mock Tudor and Elizabethan, nicknamed Tudorbethan. This hybrid style mixed traditional designs on the exterior, and the comforts of modernity such as electricity and indoor plumbing inside. However, outbreaks of Modernity did occur in this realm of wistfulness... There was also room among the mock timber for the white walled, flat roofed house. (2025)

A flat roof is usually not so good in the English rain, and reminiscent of the High and Over style in Amersham.

Ickenham, the original village that is, was noted for its church and ornamental pump and, worried about the increase in traffic, the local council asked for a maximum speed limit of 7mph to be imposed. But this wasn't recently. It was actually in 1909. How horrified the village elders would have been today. It is also concerning how the narrow lanes and rural atmosphere of Middlesex were converted, quite swiftly, into a suburban area, indistinguishable from many others. In order to do this, many old trees were felled and the lanes converted into arterial roads accompanied, on the roadside, by large steel lamps so that the sun never entirely sets on these new conglomerations. Most of the houses that were built here were semi-detached, and they were built quite speedily. There were perks attached to these new dwellings, designed to speed up sales. The basic cost was often just under £600 and, if you were lucky, the builder might throw in free fittings and even a season ticket to town, just to get you started. Most of this building occurred in the 1930s but came to a shuddering halt due to the outbreak of war in 1939. In some cases it never resumed because of the introduction of the Green Belt. The speed of creation of these suburbs due to the Met is quite remarkable but, despite my love of much of Metro-land, this building boom did destroy a massive amount of the countryside.

THE RUISLIP CONNECTION

When I grew up in the 1950s and 1960s Northwood, Middlesex, was a genteel place sullied only by one isolated unexplained death, supposedly a murder, in a flat close to the town centre. I know this because I was eventually idly looking for a place of my own, being about to spread my wings. The local medical practice was run by doctors who actually thoroughly examined you rather than trying to wean a diagnosis by sitting in front of a computer. Hands on rather than hands off, because they now appear to be afraid of catching something.

There was something very safe about Northwood. It was quite well heeled and there was little crime. It was a suburb that the designers of Metro-land could well have had in mind. There was not a lot of traffic and the gardens were generous, with each house set well away from its neighbours. It wasn't the cramped quasi-individual suburbia of Harrow but then we were further out of town, situated between what one might term basic minimum Metro-land further towards London and maximum Metro-land further out in Hertfordshire and Buckinghamshire. It was the era of cocktail parties. We owned a Yorkshire terrier at the time and unfortunately he was unable to tell the difference between the legs standing around at a cocktail party and the trees outside. So those affected could not regard him as a liquid asset in the same way as everything else on offer. On another occasion this terrier escaped and, after much searching, was found, having been picked up by the milkman and was doing the rounds on his cart.

The 1960s was a time of excellent local services. Fresh bread was provided by the baker's van, Garners, and the laundry man also attended on a regular basis. Fred the milkman, together with his two horses, Bessie and Goldie, collected the milk money every Friday and rumour had it that he put the money on the horses. Not Bessie and Goldie you understand, although they may have got the wrong idea as, one day, they bolted with the milk cart and careered down the hill towards the shops. They came to grief crashing through the glass of Green Lane Electric, although I doubt they were after a new television. The latter invention was in its infancy in this country. Bulky and prone to fault, they took hours to warm up and when they did, a feeble monochrome picture could only be controlled by banging on top of the set to stop the picture slipping. A far cry from today's technological wonders.

The period after the Second World War was one of difficulty in which families struggled to adjust to the new normality, especially in those decimated areas in London which Hitler had bombed and where the breadwinner had been a casualty of war.

My impression of school life then and of life in general was that it was much more formal. Evidenced by such things as bowler hats for city gents and where even film reviews referred to the male actors as "Mister" in their copy, and workmen referred to you formally. We seem to have drifted so far away from that now, where almost anything goes, so that as the expectations for behaviour have declined, the opportunities for crime have increased. In so doing, respect seems to have also disappeared.

One of my contemporaries from St Martin's prep school was Bruce Alexander, best known as the comically vain Superintendent Mullett in *A Touch of Frost* (1992–2010), and who I later used in a show at the Yvonne Arnaud Theatre in Guildford. He is a fine actor and also, strangely, a qualified solicitor. Well, it helps with the contracts.

The Good Life (1975–1978), or rather that part of it that was set in the back garden where much fun was had in the mud, was shot in Kewferry Road, Northwood, just a third of a mile away from where I lived in Grove Road. HMRC, in true bullying fashion, thought that the owners of the next-door property where Margo and Jerry lived had been paid some fantastic sum by the BBC. In fact it was very modest indeed, just enough for an evening out. Some years ago I was able to discuss it with her when I ran into Penelope Keith at Surrey University. This programme clearly defined the atmosphere of the time, with violence and drugs nowhere to be seen, leaving just petty bickering. It also seemed to illustrate that if you left your comfortable job in favour of being self sufficient, you were bound to be short of cash and became a pariah in terms of the suburban expectations of Metro-land. If you didn't use the train, and didn't comply with the behaviour of the weekday suits, you really were completely naff, old boy.

Northwood backed on to Ruislip. At the age of 16, a friend and I decided to enlist in a couple of horror films at a Ruislip cinema. Not yet able to drive and it being a fine night, we made our way from Northwood via Ruislip Woods, skirting the Lido with its puny pedal boats. Returning at 10.30pm and infected with visions of giant apes and haunted houses, we retraced our steps across the heathland towards Northwood. It was a strange night which I still relive with utter clarity. The moon was full, giving off a clear, silvery light which, whilst it lit our way home, also created a strange night world that Christopher Robin always loved. As we passed a hedge, a flock of birds flew up startled. It made us feel uneasy. Little did we know until getting the local paper a few days later that there was a dead body lying just behind that very hedge and not far from the water. Our evening of horror was complete.

On another occasion, I spent a week working after school at the local greengrocer's. It was highlighted by three events which I will never forget. The first was when the shop manager asked me to help a female assistant to bring out a crate of bananas from the store. As we did so, a large spider that had clearly travelled with the bananas emerged from the crate and disappeared into the sleeve of the blue uniform worn by my female colleague. She immediately dropped her end of the crate, on her foot as it happened, and broke into a sort of dance (the tarantella?) because of the pain in her foot and her newly unwanted companion. She then started a sort of impromptu striptease routine, divesting her clothing to rid herself of the black beast. Ever since then, I have always hated spiders.

On another occasion in that week, I was asked, at the end of the day, to take a single melon up to the hospital. Not being a competent driver at that time, I placed the melon on the floor of the van and drove off. As I went along, the van door started to slide open and the melon, encouraged by the vibration, headed towards the door. Rather than stop, which would have been the sensible thing to do, I bent down to try and rescue the melon. Having taken my eyes off the road, I then felt a significant bump and, horrified, I stopped. Fortunately, I found myself half on the pavement between two concrete lamp posts, the bump being my mounting of the pavement and not, fortunately, a pedestrian.

The third thing was more damaging. A lady in Moor Park was in a hurry for a delivery and I was asked late in the day to rush it to her in the van. As I left the shop, carrying the crate, I tripped over an uneven pavement and went sprawling, breaking three front teeth in the process. Bruised and unable to eat solids for a week, I was taken to the aforementioned Mr Entwhistle, and then, because he was unable to cope, dispatched to Wimpole Street for treatment via the Met. All this in just one week.

Edwards and Pilgram describe how, from the Helen Hoare Collection

The Ruislip Connection

Ruislip: All roads lead to The Poplars.

> This was Ruislip's most famous spot for refreshments and fun in the dreamy summer days, when it never rained, before 1914. "Come to breezy Ruislip, the garden of Middlesex, with its magnificent woods and splendid scenery. [Stretching a point, even then!] One can walk for miles through beautiful pasture covered with wild flowers. Toys, sweets, and high teas." The enterprising owner of The Poplars, George Weedon, had a brilliant publicity idea in 1913. He dressed the waitresses in green and white outfits, with white shoes and caps. Each girl wore an imitation flower "name" – Poppy, Rose, Violet, etc. (64, 1986)

The house stood at the junction of Ruislip High Street and Ickenham Road. Can't see him getting planning permission for this today but it was just one of the quaint enterprises that sprung up to amuse the locals who fell for them with enthusiasm. And it brought to a close that sunset era just before the First World War.

THE CHESS VALLEY AND BEYOND

The Metropolitan Line is dotted with little pieces of local history that show how far we have come to the present day in terms of old habits and traditions. Edwards and Pilgram tell us that in Chorleywood, according to the Rickmansworth Historical Society

> Ladies didn't carry the shopping home from town on the Cedars Estate 50 years ago. They telephoned their order to Mr Palmer in Rickmansworth and that very afternoon his van would come bumping out over the new, wide estate roads along the valley to deliver fresh butter, cheese, Chivers Jellies and packets of Mazawattee Tea. (84, 1986)

Now we have to make do with Waitrose. Mazawattee Tea incidentally hails from China as long ago as 1887 and was imported by the Densham family. After all, tea drinking had its origin in China rather than India.

John Betjeman draws our attention in *Metro-land* to the house built by Charles Voysey in the very early 20th century, a house where

> all must be plain and practical. The sloping buttress walls to counteract the outward thrust of the heavy slate roof. The stepped tiles below the chimney pots are there to throw off the driving English rain... And wood smoke mingled with the sulphur fumes and people could catch the early train to London and be home just after tea. (1973)

Because the Voyseys were rather short, the proportions inside the house reflect this, rather a surprise after the outside. Nevertheless, it provided a template for many other houses in that area of the Chilterns. It predated the Cedars Estate by nearly 20 years and the emphasis, as with so much of Metro-land, was on preserving the natural world as far as possible so that these houses seemed part of the local countryside rather than an intrusion. Today they can fetch vast sums and, even at the time, a substantial property could set you back £3,250, although there were smaller ones for rather less than £750. And if you add to that the cost of commuting which, after all, was what the Met was about, you would be looking at just above £75 for an annual season, actually about one tenth of the value of the smallest house. But, given the prospect of surrounding village greens and woods, it was a remarkably good bargain. This was the real heart of Metro-land.

According to Buckinghamshire County Museum

> The Chilterns were sprinkled by great beechwoods [hence Beaconsfield] in which individual craftsmen, known as bodgers, worked away amongst the fresh timber on improvised lathes, turning out a vast assortment of wooden products. Their work would be collected, and perhaps assembled finally in the village before being taken to the London markets – often by Metropolitan goods train. (94, 1986)

We have now rather forgotten the countless crafts that used to take place in the woods, and the idea of a bodger nowadays has changed its meaning to someone who does not carry out his chosen task properly, when originally it meant a modest, country worker.

It seems to me that when steam finally died out on the Met beyond Rickmansworth and out to Aylesbury on 9 September 1961, this somehow marked the end of the line for the rag and bone man, the milkman with his horses and other street suppliers of the past. It was as if electrification of the railway swept away the old traditions that gave individuality to the area, with the past replaced by, in the worst cases, a numbingly bland suburbia. Whereas I admire what the Met achieved in a remarkably short time, the leaflets extolling the Metro-land countryside were a feeble attempt, in their flowery prose, to laud what the development of the railway had done much to destroy. The countryside so described is more of a re-imagination of a bucolic distant past that no longer exists, and probably never did. Looking back on it now, my childhood seems to have been in another country, very different from the hard-edged commercialism that pervades everything today. They do things differently there.

We have largely forgotten the emphasis on work that persisted up to the Second World War and a little beyond. Many people had little time for leisure because their time off was spent recovering from one working week, often including Saturdays, while preparing for another. The ludicrous concept of working from home, which has been allowed to weaken our resolve as a country, would have been laughed out of court. The only advantage that the London Saturday workers had then was a more relaxed dress code in contrast to the weekly suits and bowlers, plus the opportunity to catch the Saturday lunchtime Pullman, an American concept, which offered the rare opportunity for food and drink on the way home. But the railways now, including the Met, have frowned on such individuality, just as they have removed all the named express trains. In doing so, the pride of the railways has disappeared in favour of disconnected companies, some foreign owned, who do not give a damn about the service. France's SNCF may be the complete opposite but, despite some difficulties, there is a great deal to admire.

The Leventon family lived in Chorleywood and had an artistic bent; Annabel became an actress while her mother used to teach singing, rather strictly I recall, to the boys at St Martin's prep school. She was to the then pupils what the late Barbara Woodhouse was to dogs. I was one of the unfortunates. In time, she was replaced by the saturnine Mr Gibson, who used to keep a gym shoe on the piano to remind his charges just what would happen if you did not conform. These days it would not be allowed. No idle threats of that nature would be tolerated. Today the lunatics run the asylum if they can make up their minds what sex they are out of a substantial choice. But are they any happier? I rather doubt it.

One of the still-delightful places that can be explored by hopping off the Met at Chalfont and Latimer, and well away from the busy main drag of ribbon development, is the Chess Valley, which affords delightful views as the River Chess winds its way along the valley floor, its source in nearby Chesham. Once you get out beyond the M25, there are some wonderful places to be explored. In a small country where so much has been ruined by development, the Chess Valley is barely a mile from the horrors of the Amersham to Chalfont main road. I say "horrors" because the last time I used it, it was pockmarked by a series of extraordinarily dangerous potholes so that you had to keep steering to the wrong side of the road to avoid them. Disgraceful for an A road to have been allowed to fall into this condition. It created the strange feeling of driving up a country track somehow misplaced to a built-up area.

Once upon a time the local councils were the servants of the community and were paid accordingly. Now their CEOs believe themselves to be business leaders, unwisely spending the people's hard-earned cash both on themselves and in unwise investments in Iceland and elsewhere. The results of such strategy are painfully obvious. Whereas the Victorians once led the way developing industry and architecture, we are now ruled by incompetent politicians and company execs who seem to lack all flair in disproportion to their ludicrously high salaries. Matthew Engel confirms this in *Eleven Minutes Late: A Train Journey to the Soul of Britain*.

> A high speed rail map of Europe is already taking shape. Britain is represented by one remote spur, the line optimistically known as High Speed 1, connecting London to the Channel Tunnel, a mere 205 years after the idea of a tunnel was first mooted…
>
> One must allow for… the weary fearfulness that affects a governing class with a long record of disastrous management of major public projects; and the temptations of short-termism that inevitably afflict here-today gone-tomorrow politicians…
>
> Britain has never been able to reconcile the past and the future. That's the disaster. (29/30, 2009)

The Chess Valley has a rather special, rather superior feel to it, this despite the ghastly potholes that chequer its country lanes. I want to start by looking at Chenies. According to *Chenies, a brief history of the village*,

> Chenies village lies in the very eastern part of south Buckinghamshire. It is situated to the east of Chesham and the Chalfonts. Chenies is also a civil parish within Chiltern district. Until the 13th century, the village name was Isenhampstead.
>
> There were two villages here, called Isenhampstead Chenies and Isenhampstead Latimers, distinguished by the lords of the manors of those two places. In the 19th century the prefix was dropped and the two villages became known as Chenies and Latimer. Near the village there was once a royal hunting-box, where King Edward I and King Edward II were known to have resided. It was the owner of this lodge, Edward III's shield bearer, Thomas Cheyne, who first gave his name to the village and his descendant, Sir John Cheyne, who built Chenies Manor House in around 1460 on this site. (2025)

The original name of Isenhampstead was Saxon in origin and it was first mentioned in 1165 when the owner was a knight by the name of Alexander de Isenhampstead, who may have been the ancestor of Alexander Cheyne who resided there in the 13th century. Isen, incidentally, is a municipality in the district of Erding, Bavaria, where there was once a Benedictine abbey. Once again the Church was in the background, controlling.

Derek Ayshford tells us that there was probably a wooden church that predated the current one on the site of St Michael's.

> In 1526 John Russell married the heiress to the Cheyney estate and became the village's most notable personality. The owner of a small Dorset estate and a gifted linguist he had the good fortune to be presented to Henry VII, who made him a gentleman usher – the first step to an earldom and the great Bedford fortune. (2025)

After that there was no stopping him and, under Henry VIII, he became Lord High Admiral of England as well as serving under both Edward VI and Mary I as Lord Privy Seal.

> It is said that his portrait shows a man who was cautious, prudent and thoughtful and he must indeed have been to serve four Tudor monarchs and to die peacefully in his bed! (1987)
>
> Russell oversaw enlargements to the manor so that he could entertain Henry VIII. Because he so loved the village, he asked to be buried in the local church.
>
> This his widow arranged and built the Chapel in which all the subsequent Earls and Dukes have been buried up to the present time. At the same time that the manor was enlarged the village grew and became considerably bigger than it is today, though there are still several timber framed cottages dating from this period. (2025)
>
> Much later, in 1829, the Rev. Lord Wriothesley Russell came to be Rector of Chenies. He was the youngest son of the 6th Duke of Bedford. Arriving when he was just 25, he remained in the village until his death in 1886. The Church offered him high office but he refused, stating he wished to remain with his village flock. He was an admirably modest fellow, despite his background, and before the school was built, he taught the local children to read and write in the Rectory kitchen.
>
> He refused to have a new carpet in his study as the men would not like to walk on it in their boots. The affection in which he was held is attested to by the lovely illuminated address, with its charming watercolour scenes, which still hangs in the church. The address was presented to the Rector by the villagers to mark his 50th anniversary as their priest. On each side of the address may be seen the signatures

of the donors – said to include the whole village. It is interesting that some of these names are still to be found either in the village or the surrounding area. (2025)

Chenies was once known for its paper mills, such as Dodds, powered by the nearby River Chess. Nearby is the parish church of St Michael and its adjoining Bedford Chapel, which contains the burial places of many of the Russell family. It is situated close to the manor house, which was often the norm at that time. Apparently, the collection of tombs to the Russells, the Dukes of Bedford, is one of the finest to be found anywhere in England. The nearby pub, The Bedford Arms, continues the name to this day. When the Duke of Bedford's estate was sold in 1954, this area was split off and acquired by a property developer who wanted to put up lots of tacky houses. Fortunately for this rather smart place this was not permitted, and the local properties which had previously been rented out to the Duke's tenants were then sold to them. Accordingly, many of the farms in the area continued unabashed, although some of them have since become private residences in a move towards the gentrification of the area. I am pleased to say that, although Chenies has inevitably altered over time, it still retains its special character, with the vast and imposing chimneys that dignify the manor house and one or two other local properties. The area has a superior feel.

Ayshford tells us that

> The larger houses provided work for both men and women. The village blacksmith shod horses and repaired farm machinery. Bread was baked locally and the necessities of life could be bought in the village shops. (2025)

Mechanisation inevitably brought about change: agricultural labourers were thrown off the land as the old system of strip farming, which had brought some basic employment to many, was replaced by larger farms based on economies of scale. These labourers were forced to find work elsewhere and even abroad. When many ended up in nearby towns, the village lost its self sufficiency and many shops closed, the last one being the post office in 1975. So when, in 1954, the Duke of Bedford sold the Chenies estate to cover death duties, there was an irrevocable split between the Woburn estate and the village, although the family still maintain an interest, particularly in the Bedford Chapel, where so many of their ancestors lie.

One of the best views can be obtained from the garden of Latimer House, once an important historical centre and now an indifferent De Vere Hotel. It seems a shame that the current owners have not done more to maximise this splendid building with its remarkable heavy-duty chimneys. While the public areas are still naturally splendid, the bedrooms are mostly disappointing unless you choose from the top of the range. The superior rooms are anything but, resembling shoe boxes with inadequate natural light. However, the bar leads on to a splendid terrace area where one can pleasantly while away the summer evenings with a great view of both the garden and the river beyond. There may even be a deliberately blocked-up secret area left over from the war. Latimer House was built on the top of a hill overlooking the picturesque Latimer village. It originated as a home for the Cavendish family, the home of the barons Chesham. Curiously, the family had to decamp to Latimer House when Chatsworth was temporarily sequestered by Parliament in the 17th century. Something of a comedown.

According to Wikipedia

> During the Second World War, the house was the headquarters of IV Corps from August 1940, and the centre of top secret activities by MI5 and MI6. It was also one of three stately homes where captured German U-boat submarine crews and Luftwaffe pilots were initially held before being transferred to conventional prisoner of war camps. The centre included M Room, with special recording equipment, and the covert approach was kept in secret, even from Parliament. They recorded private conversations between German prisoners and Generals, giving away war secrets in the process. (2025)

From this, useful information was gleaned about Hitler's VI and V2 rockets which may have contributed to saving many lives. Latimer House may not be as well known as Bletchley Park but played an equally important role.

> When the estate was sold in the 1980s, a clause was added by the government to not open a secret wall in the basement for the next 50 years, as it also hides a secret tunnel used for top secret activities. (2025)

In 1953, after the death of the 4th Baron Chesham, the house became the HQ of the National Defence College. At 9.10am on 12 February

1974, a bomb planted by the IRA detonated, injuring ten people but not killing anyone. The cost of the damage was about £6,000. Now, of course, a hotel, I doubt if many of the guests give much thought to the chequered past of this interesting building.

Another smaller point of interest is the Liberty Tomb, to be found close to the Chess Valley footpath and dedicated to "William Liberty, a free thinker". He died in 1777 and expressed the wish to be buried alone but near his mansion, which no longer exists. Presumably it was not called Liberty Hall. The inscription reads

> Sacred to the memory of Mr William Liberty of Chorleywood. Brickmaker who was by his own desire buried in a vault in this part of his estate. He died 21st April 1777 aged 52 years. Here also lieth the body of Alice Liberty widower [?] of the above named William Liberty who died 29th May 1809 aged 72 years.

William was related to the family who owned Liberty's in Regent Street. I am grateful to Chenies Village website (2025) for the above information. Coming across the tomb for the first time renders it something of a surprise, but it is a fine backdrop in which to be laid to rest even if the incumbents are blind to its treasures. A reminder of our own mortality, it acts as a sobering thought as you continue up the footpath towards Chesham. At least the footpath keeps you free from those appalling potholes that haunt the roads in the area.

Chesham still manages to maintain a sense of the ethos of Metro-land despite having become much busier in the intervening years. It has done so in a way that the old market town of Aylesbury has not, the latter having grown into a vast uncontrolled sprawl. It might be imagined that the town is named after the River Chess, but in fact the reverse is true. The old English name from which Chesham derives is Caestaelshamm, which means "the river meadow at the pile of stones". It was first mentioned in the will of Lady Ælfigu, ex-wife of King Eadwig. Up until 1066 three estates were associated with what was now known as Caestrehamm, and these are recorded in the Domesday Book. The most important of these manors was that held by Lady Edith, the widow of Edward the Confessor. Incidentally, this and the previous entry give the lie to the idea that women had no control at this time. They very clearly did, and could exercise substantial influence. Other estates included that of Harold Godwinson and his brother, Leofwine. Part of these became Chesham Bois, and post 1066, Edith was allowed to keep her lands while William the Conqueror divided other estates between his half-brother, Bishop Odo of Bayeux and Hugh de Bolbec. I am grateful to Wikipedia 2025 for this information; just a small part of the long and fascinating history of this town.

Chesham was once known for its four Bs – boots, beer, brushes and Baptists according to Wikipedia.

> In the face of fierce competition from both home and abroad during the late 19th and early 20th centuries, the three traditional industries rapidly declined. (2025)

However, making use of skilled labour, new industries grew up in the years before the Second World War, including light industry, professional services and technology.

There is evidence of settlement here from 5000BC, the Late Mesolithic period, from which a number of flint tools have been found. This was followed by farming in the Neolithic era, around two and a half thousand years later, Bronze Age settlement in 1800bc and Iron Age Belgic people around 500bc. Then came the Romans who farmed here between ad 150 and 400, after which there appears to have been a gap until the 7th century.

Before the 13th century, the three Cestreham manors were known as Chesham Higham, Chesham Bury and Chesham Bois. In the 14th century they were first recorded as "the manors of Great Chesham". Collectively they extended beyond the Chesham town boundary. Together with the manor at Latimer they were held by the Earls of Oxford and Surrey. During the 16th century Greater Chesham was owned by the Seymour family, who disposed of it to the Cavendish family, the Earls and later Dukes of Devonshire. It is from the 15th century that the earliest surviving properties survive, found close by the church in an area called *the Nap*, and along part of the present-day Church Street. Though gradually disposing of land, the Cavendishes maintained an influence in the town until the 19th century. The Lowndes family started purchasing land from the 16th century, William Lowndes being an influential politician (2025).

Chesham has a reputation for religious dissent and in 1532, Thomas Harding was burnt at the stake for being a Lollard (a follower of John Wycliffe) and a heretic. The Lollards believed that the Church should help people imitate Christ by leading a life of evangelical poverty. Chesham became a focus for dissenters from the approved religion, even if they were not as unlucky as Harding.

An inspiring Metro-land poster encouraging the reader to both use and buy property on the line, 1914. (Source: Lordprice Collection, Alamy)

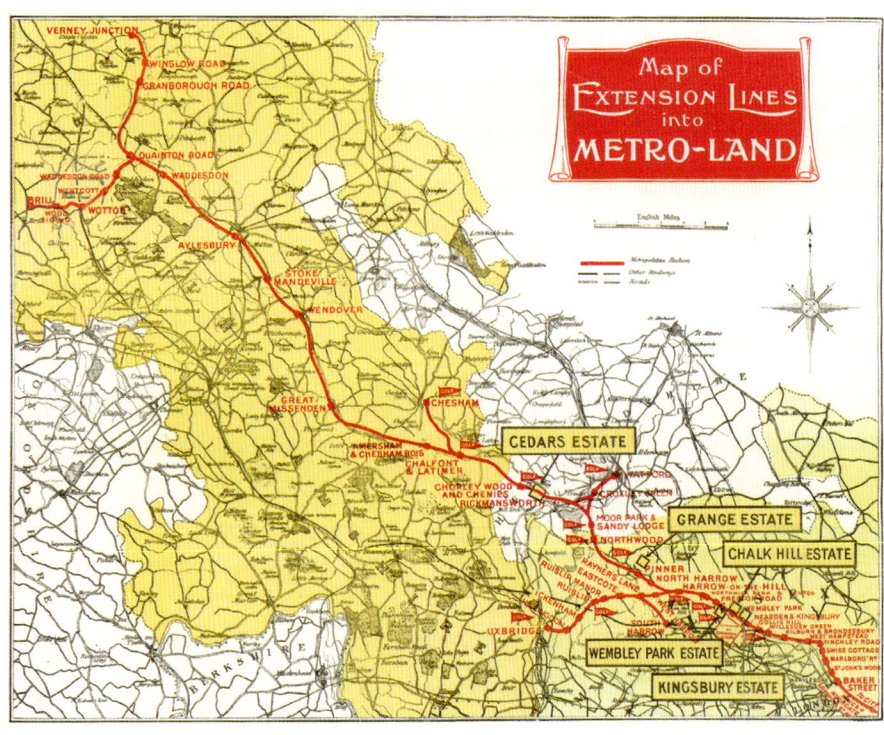

A map of Metro-land, the residential area in London's northwest hinterland served by London's Metropolitan Line. (Source: Alamy)

Striking advertisements and posters for the Metropolitan Line. (Source: Alamy)

Batchworth Heath Lodge at the entrance to Moor Park Golf Club. (Source: Kemp, W.A.G., The Story of Northwood and Northwood Hills, Middlesex; Publisher: W.A.G. Kemp,1955)

Joel Street railway bridge just prior to the building of Northwood Hills station. (Source: Kemp, W.A.G., The Story of Northwood and Northwood Hills, Middlesex; Publisher: W.A.G. Kemp,1955)

The origin of Northwood lies with The Grange, an ancient house first occupied by monks. (Source: Kemp, W.A.G., The Story of Northwood and Northwood Hills, Middlesex; Publisher: W.A.G. Kemp,1955)

Metropolitan No 1. An early tank engine used to pull rolling stock prior to electrification. (Source: Wikimedia Commons, creative commons licence)

Sarah Siddons, a Bo-bo electric locomotive still going after more than a hundred years. (Source: Wikimedia Commons, creative commons licence; credit: kitmasterbloke)

The latest model electric train S7+1. (Source: Wikimedia Commons, creative commons licence)

Metropolitan Line silver rolling stock. (Source: Wikimedia Commons, creative commons licence)

Amersham station after a night of snow. (Source: Wikimedia Commons, creative commons licence; credit: Dean Mitchell)

Site of Marlborough Road station appearing in John Betjeman's Metro-land. (Source: Wikimedia Commons, creative commons licence; credit: Oxyman)

Verney Junction station in the 1960s. (Source: Wikimedia Commons, creative commons licence; credit: Lamberhurst)

A steam hauled train passing Waddesdon Manor station. (Source: Wikimedia Commons, creative commons licence; credit: A Cherry of Waddesdon)

Madeleine Fletcher, a long-time resident of Chesham and the nearby area, has the following memory:

> As a child I lived right next to the Little Chalfont/Chesham line which of course was built as a result of the Met. (Quill Hall Lane, Amersham). At the time we had steam trains puffing up and down, mum could only put the washing out at certain times! The verges would catch fire on occasion and some nights we were kept awake due to maintenance on the track. It changed in the sixties (I think) when it went electric of course. We missed the old puffer but not the sooty air.
>
> I didn't get to take a journey on this line until years later after moving to Chesham to our beautiful quiet cottage. I remember the first time when I was able to catch sight of how close my childhood home was to the track. (2025)

By a stroke of good fortune, she has lived with her husband in this cottage just outside Chesham for more than 50 years, a fairy dingle where the open field opposite has somehow escaped being built on. The cottage was not, of course, a Met Line build but it plainly echoes the finest sentiments to which Metro-land aspires and, in Madeleine's case, the cottage and its garden have become a lifelong pleasure.

The Chesham branch line from Chalfont and Latimer marks the end of the Metropolitan Line, and in John Betjeman's 1973 film *Metro-land*, it is this branch, rather than the main line at Amersham, that is chosen to terminate the high-speed cab journey up the Met that dominates the start of this excellent film. It seems a curious decision when the line originally stretched beyond Aylesbury to Verney Junction.

Amersham-on-the-Hill, now the terminal for Met trains, is an extraordinarily busy town with little parking, situated above the long hill that stretches down through Chesham Bois and on to Chesham. It grew naturally out of the growth of the railway along with accompanying suburbia. I have tried to like it but I can't. It seems a merely functional dormitory town where the chances of being mown down whilst trying to cross the road are higher than usual. On one occasion, I literally had to fling myself against the bank on the far side of the road to avoid being run over by an expensive BMW driver who refused to slow down, let alone stop. It seems to sum up all that is wrong with Amersham-on-the-Hill. It is about money and what it does to people.

I used to attend a dentist (yes, another one!) in Amersham called Mr Jones, and got used to seeing him in his surgery. One day I was in a car showroom and in walks Mr Jones. I was quite unreasonably outraged. So strongly had I associated person and place that I felt that Mr Jones could and should only be seen in his surgery and never outside it. He should have been locked in at night so that he could never leave. Or perhaps I should.

At the other end of the Met, in Wimpole Street, I was temporarily in the hands of a private dentist who, surprisingly, gave his patients general anaesthetic on the basis he could treat them more efficiently if they were out cold. On one occasion I agreed to act as a patient for him (free of charge) in a demonstration for students, and found myself being treated in a boxing ring surrounded by a huge number of enquiring faces. I suppose this was an appropriate place to be knocked out, medically speaking, but I would not like to repeat it. However, the dentist, a kindly Scot, was eventually attacked for his methods in a nasty article, resulting in a high-profile legal case. He was never the same again and general anaesthetic was never adopted for general dental practice as it were considered too risky. However, it was dreamily pleasant to wake up to a pretty nurse peering into your face and asking after you. Also, you were pretty wobbly afterwards and couldn't go home on your own. So maybe it was for the best. However, he was a courteous man and a very careful dentist, and he did not deserve this. End of Met-based dental stories and my obsession with them.

By comparison continue down the hill on the south side where Amersham old town is a relative delight, even if one end of it has been wrecked by an enormous and unsightly Tesco. What were the planners thinking in allowing this? However, the area north-west of the market square contains rows of old cottages interspersed by public houses of indifferent quality. If you can find a place to park your car, assuming it is still in one piece after all the potholes, you can stray off the main drag and inspect the church and the graveyard where lies Ruth Ellis, the last woman to be hanged.

However, I understand that the tunnel for HS2 has been driven underneath Old Amersham. It remains to be seen what this will do to the old buildings above. There is also a Grade II listed market hall to be considered.

According to the Amersham Society (2025), it was known as Elmodesham in AD796, and as Agmodesham in the Domesday survey of 1086. In 1200, King John granted a charter for a weekly market and annual fair. Two Members of Parliament were then chosen to represent the town. Situated on the banks of the River Misbourne, Old Amersham, or more correctly Amersham, more satisfactorily fulfils the aspirations of Metro-land than its ugly sister up the hill.

Just outside the town towards Great Missenden lies Shardeloes, a country house dating from the mid-18th century. It was built for William Drake, the MP for Amersham. According to Wikipedia 2025, the architect was the wonderfully named Stiff Leadbetter (no jokes please!), who also oversaw the construction. Like the mansion at Moor Park, it is built in the Palladian style of stuccoed brick, and the roof is largely hidden by a balustrade. Interestingly, the original plans show a design similar to Holkham Hall in Norfolk, which was cancelled in favour of Robert Adam's plans for the interior. There is also fine ornamental plasterwork.

> The house is flanked to the west by a service block and stable yard of the same period as the mansion, complete with clock tower. (Wikipedia, 2025)

Humphrey Repton was responsible for laying out the grounds and dammed the River Misbourne in order to achieve a lake. The word is that the tunnelling for HS2 may have caused some damage to this. The estate also includes a cricket ground, the home ground of Amersham Cricket Club.

At one point it looked as if the house, ancestral home of the Tyrwhitt-Drake family, might fall to demolition as it was in a poor state after the war, during which it served as a maternity hospital where, apparently, three thousand children were born. However, thanks to a concerted campaign by the Council for the Protection of Rural England and the Amersham Society, it was preserved and turned into flats by property developer Richard Watson. Amongst its tenants were the late husband and wife actors Michael Denison and Dulcie Gray, natural bastions of Metro-land whose genteel presentation never varied between different productions, which usually included a sofa.

From the above, it can be seen that these fine houses were dotted throughout Metro-land, particularly in Hertfordshire and Buckinghamshire, and it seems curious to me that the Metropolitan Line literature concentrates mainly on farming, golfing and the countryside rather than mentioning some of its finest jewels. Surely these would have made an excellent selling point for those looking to purchase new property in the area. Instead, the brochures point to a curious rural idyll that might have been more familiar to Shakespeare's contemporaries than the modern society it was aimed at. There is a lack of realism about the flowery prose that invites the punter into a kind of Never Never Land which seems more appropriate to Peter Pan. Yet despite this, the blurb clearly worked and the interweaving of the railway's development with new property on its periphery could be considered a major success.

Around the age of 20 and, as a recently qualified driver, I made, as it turned out, the mistaken decision to try and better myself by asking out the daughter of a wealthy shoe retailer of the time. So, climbing aboard my newish Ford Anglia we headed out into the balmy summer evening air of the Chilterns. All appeared to be going well but my newly found confidence was short lived. After a while, she looked witheringly at the car and then at me and said: "I hope this car has a petrol gauge. I wouldn't want to be stuck out here in the country with you."

Needless to say, I returned her safely to her parents without further delay. I never viewed my Ford Anglia in the same light again.

POINTS WEST

For a while I worked in Marlow, a stylish but busy town on the banks of the Thames, much beloved of authors and film makers. Best known for The Compleat Angler hotel, it is perhaps technically outside what most people would think of as Metro-land, and certainly anything on the south side of the river would not really qualify. Yet it strongly conveys the ethos envisioned by the creators of Metro-land even if the distance to the nearest Met Line station is a bit of a stretch. But then what I am trying to convey to the reader is a sense of place, and as the early literature suggests, I can draw my own boundaries.

The Thames is not a large river by world standards, winding its way from its source in Gloucestershire through some spectacular Buckinghamshire valleys through the capital to its quite impressive estuary on the east coast. To those west of London it is a favourite for boating, while for Londoners, it can't quite shake off the horrors of Dickens. Towards the mouth it becomes a gateway for onward adventure suggested by Conrad in his novella *Heart of Darkness* (1899), even though Conrad was mainly Polish and didn't speak English until his early 20s.

But we are concerned only with the western section as a boundary and only a relatively small part of that, keeping in mind perhaps both *The Wind in the Willows* (1908) and Jerome's *Three Men in a Boat* (1889). Both of these suggest idling one's time away on the river and its periphery, although the latter occasionally suggests something a little darker. Incidentally, you can get a most splendid view of the Thames from the magnificent Danesfield House Hotel, where I once worked temporarily for a private company before it became a hotel. It is a little pompous but its grand position well above the river justifies it, even if a cup of coffee will set you back rather more than expected. Its 60 acres figure in Jerome's book, and the name derives from its site as an encampment for the Danes, as mentioned in *TMIAB*. I see no real difference between the petty squabbling of Kenneth Grahame's characters and those of Jerome. They have both chosen the river as an idyllic setting to idle away the time in the same way that the creators of Metro-land desired their new home owners to utilise their weekends, recharging their batteries for the upcoming week's work. The late John Mortimer set his serial *Paradise Postponed* (1986) close to this rich area, in Turville and Henley, and if you can get hold of a copy of the video, you will admire the strong sense of place. So now I want to select two properties as examples along the banks of the river, one good and one bad.

The first of these can be found between Marlow and Henley and is located down a country lane. It is the rather wonderful Medmenham Abbey. Nancy Bilyeau tells us that

> History does not record a single event of interest that took place within the abbey while Cistercian monks actually inhabited the abbey between 1204 and 1536. It's what happened to a woman around the time of its founding and to a man 200 years after its dissolution that spark interest – and in the case of what happened in the 18th century, a notoriety that lasts up to today. (2018)

The woman in question was Isabel de Bolebec and, no doubt, a French speaker. She granted lands to the abbey at Woburn, and they immediately decided to take advantage. Medmenham Abbey was originally her father's house and so the lands in question were those between the manor and the Thames. She had done a great deal for the Catholic Church in England, particularly with regard to the Dominicans. Thus the Cistercians, or at least a section of them, began to live in their newly constructed abbey on the Thames. And what a beautiful site it is, set in the rolling hills between Marlow and Henley. It may seem extraordinary to us but

> In 1206, Isabel's husband died, and she petitioned King John for the right to not be married again or, if she did, to choose the man herself. She was about 40 years of age. Nearly all marriages of heiresses were arranged, with their fortunes as rich prizes for the king to bestow on men he wished to favour... Henry I is known to have charged rich widows for the privilege of remaining single. Sometimes the woman had to pay the king in order to release back to them their own inheritances! (2018)

Isabel paid King John 300 marks and three horses (or palfreys) just for the right to marry the man of her choice. He turned out to be Robert de Vere, about her own age and from a family as old as her own. They very quickly had a son, Hugh, and her husband eventually inherited the title of Earl of Oxford. The de Veres held on to this title until 1703, all directly descended from Isabel.

The Cistercians were not so lucky when, with the dissolution of the monasteries, Medmenham, one of the smaller ones, was broken up. However, in 1536 only the abbot and one monk lived there; they were of course evicted, with the abbot receiving a pension of 10 marks.

Henry VII granted the stone buildings and land to Thomas and Robert More. After that it passed to the Duffield family who eventually leased it to Sir Francis Dashwood. We could consider the two owners polar opposites. We may associate the notorious Hellfire Club with the caves under the church at West Wycombe, some miles away, but it was not confined to one location.

Bilyeau tells us that

> By the age of 18, Dashwood was a prominent member of the Dilletanti Society, devoted to celebrating the values of ancient Rome and Greece. He spent a great deal of money turning his father's country estate, West Wycombe Park, into an Italianate villa that eventually became known as one of the most beautiful houses in England.
>
> He was obsessed with private societies, and in 1752 he formed what he dubbed the Brotherhood of St Francis of Wycombe with like-minded friends such as the Earl of Sandwich. He soon decided that a discreet location was needed, and Dashwood poured money into Medmenham Abbey, which was near Wycombe Park. The abbey was easy to reach from London. (2018)

So what had once been an outpost of the Cistercians, devoted to prayer, now became a location devoted to dissolute behaviour. The abbey was altered in faux-Gothic style and the prevailing ethos was clearly exhibited in the stained-glass window at the entrance: *Do What You Will*. Eventually this group described themselves as the Monks of Medmenham, although anything further from the genuine article could not be imagined. Another change of name eventually occurred: the Hellfire Club. Alleged members included some extremely prominent people, including Frederick, Prince of Wales, the Duke [Marquess?] of Queensberry and even, once, Benjamin Franklin.

We cannot be certain exactly went on at these meetings, but the likelihood is that it was considerably more than political discussion and drunkenness, and rather more about debauchery, with these aristocrats involved in anti-Christian rituals and prostitutes. Despite being staunchly anti-Catholic, Dashwood and his friends were largely made up of government opposition, which gives the group a political edge. The supposition is that the club was made up of elements of all these things.

Despite employing much local labour, Dashwood and Sandwich once released a monkey into the local parish church, causing chaos and forcing the congregation to flee. It seems that Dashwood, who only held Medmenham Abbey under lease, eventually thought it better to take the Club to a more discreet location and dug out caves under the church at West Wycombe. Stories of his gross behaviour were legion, yet, amazingly, Dashwood still rose to become Chancellor of the Exchequer, despite his remarkable lack of knowledge regarding the country's finances. Something he shares with Rachel from Accounts.

We are not told whether these reports reached the ear of the Duffield family, who owned the lease. It is difficult to imagine how they could not have known, but they took back the abbey and sold it to the Chief Justice of Chester. Around 1898, the abbey was restored again, by a Mr Hudson, and it was later owned by an army colonel. While Medmenham Manor is still a highly desirable property facing the Thames, nothing remains of the abbey; just as well, one might say, given its chequered history, and while Francis Dashwood sounds like a character from a cheap novel, he certainly added some colour to the otherwise peaceful banks of the Thames. Like so many, he appeared to think that his position in life justified anything he chose to do. In his dying days, I wonder if he had cause to regret it.

And this brings us neatly to another point about Metro-land, the sense that it was designed for working people who knew how to behave. Not that the subject of religion is ever raised. Everything about the promotion of Metro-land points in this direction, a tranquil well behaved place for them to live after a hard-working week in the smoke, rather than indulge in squalid behaviour in underground caves. It was a suburban/country idyll to aspire to.

Further west lies the historic property of Cliveden, once the country seat of the Villiers family and now owned by the National Trust with a section leased out as a luxury hotel, although not the sort of hotel that appeals to me, with its often flashy clientele and mindless influencers, where money talks and you are judged by your level of conspicuous expenditure.

The site was originally owned by the 2nd Duke of Buckingham, who acquired it in 1666. With its prime position above the river, and consisting of 160 acres, the Duke had some grand plans for it. According to the National Trust

> A favourite of King Charles II, the Duke wanted a residence close to London, at which he could entertain his mistress, the Duchess of Shrewsbury, and his friends in style. Enjoying a commanding position on a chalk cliff, the name Cliff-dene was given to the estate.
> Buckingham chose a site for his house with far-reaching views above the River Thames. The land sloped steeply and massive amounts of earth were excavated and were moved from the north to the south side to create the 400ft-long platform that today we call the Parterre.
> William Winde, Buckingham's architect, created a terrace that has formed the foundations of the two subsequent houses at Cliveden and, although altered over time, much of Buckingham's design remains. (2025)

Many years later, in 1696, the house was bought by Lord George Hamilton, Earl of Orkney, who held it for 14 years. For some reason he felt that Cliveden was too tall, and ten years later, he had the top storey removed which reduced the height by some 20 feet. He also oversaw the creation of two service areas which were connected to the main house. At the end of 1723 he turned the great platform below the terrace into a grass lawn with elevated walks on either side, and called it his "quaker parterre". But he went a great deal further than this.

> Working with designer Charles Bridgeman, Orkney laid out paths running through a "formal wilderness" that stretched across the cliff tops and built an amphitheatre at the northern end of the garden. Orkney commissioned garden buildings from the Venetian designer, Giacomo Leoni, including the Blenheim Pavilion around 1727… and the Octagon Temple in 1735. (2025)

Having worked immensely hard to achieve much that is good about this estate, Orkney died in 1737 and the estate passed via the female line, for three generations. For 14 years the property was then leased to others, including the aforementioned Frederick, Prince of Wales.

In 1795, and while the Countess of Orkney was in residence, a fire burnt out the central block. Not to be done down, she continued to live there but the property was not restored until its purchase by George Warrender in 1824. He commissioned William Burn to help in the redesign so that

Cliveden was restored to its former glory. However, Cliveden's luck was out, for the central block, on which so much care and attention had been lavished, once again burnt to the ground in 1849 while the property was under the ownership of the Duchess of Sutherland, who was using it as a country retreat. The Duchess was closely allied with Queen Victoria.

Once again, an architect, Charles Barry, was brought in to redesign the central area; in 1862 a ball was held for 200 people to celebrate the completion of the three-storey Italianate villa that we know today. Barry also provided additional rooms in the single-storey wings linked to the main house by curved corridors. I am grateful to the National Trust for much of the above information.

In its long and chequered history Cliveden became the Duchess of Connaught Red Cross Hospital during the First World War, while the Astors, William Waldorf and Nancy, had ownership from 1893. Nancy was known to have worked incredibly hard to assist those patients who had so selflessly served their country. Incredibly, about 24,000 people were treated there, utilising the best conditions available at the time, with a memorial garden created for the deceased. The hospital was open until 1985, having, at its peak, been visited by royalty and other dignitaries. It was perhaps Cliveden's finest hour, and when it was eventually demolished it was replaced by environmentally friendly new homes.

Despite all their hard work, the Astors still found time to hold some glittering parties for both political leaders and those at the top of their game in art and literature, although the nature of these changed to something more serious in the run up to the Second World War.

Matters took a downturn in 1963 when, after a severe winter, John Profumo, Secretary of State for War, was forced to reveal an affair with Christine Keeler, a 19-year-old good-time girl, especially involving the swimming pool at Cliveden. After an initial cover-up failed, the enormous press exposure brought about the downfall of the Conservative government. There are two things to be said about this. Firstly, such goings-on today would be most unlikely to have the same effect, and secondly, it is worth noting that Profumo, despite his disgrace, afterwards worked tirelessly for charity until his death. A character plus that he shares with the late US President, Jimmy Carter.

And so we are back where we started, and Cliveden exists today partly as a luxury hotel and one of the visual splendours of Metro-land. At this point you will be asking me why I have made such a point of singling out the great houses of Metro-land for special mention when I have also been quite definite in singling out the concept as somewhere for the working man to live and relax, even if that species is made up of several levels, from the humble semi-dweller to the managerial types who can choose something much more exclusive, their lives largely hidden behind wrought-iron gates.

There is a relatively simple answer to that. The great houses that I have so far identified are really the crown jewels of the area and existed sometimes hundreds of years before the idea of Metro-land came into being. For the most part these houses were not there to accept the relatively humble workers envisaged by the railway. But the principle for the occupants of the great houses was not dissimilar. They, almost without exception, wanted a property that was within easy reach of London even if, at the time of occupation, that reach meant travelling by horse and carriage rather than the Met. Obviously the lives of these residents were mostly far grander and exclusive but, just as we have to accept those members of the population who never get past first base, we should also accept that there are those who, whether by favour or good fortune, have the means to look after those houses, with their long and sometimes tumultuous history. That Metro-land is full of such houses, even if some of them no longer exist, is proof that it was selected as a fine area to set up home and to bring up children. Particularly amongst the rolling hills of the Chilterns, there is a rich history of English life laid out before us as a kind of pageant to be enjoyed and, just as the concept of Metro-land is now well over a hundred years old, it has become just another part of the history of this fine area. It was already undergoing change in my childhood, with the loss of the Great Central, dual tracking of the Met Line between Harrow and Rickmansworth, and the electrification of the line out to Amersham and Chesham. While Metro-land itself has started to fade into the past due to overbuilding, we should remember that it simply kickstarted a new era of change for the working man, which has continued to this day. All this book can do is act as a 2025 snapshot of how it was then, and look back to how it all began.

IN SEARCH OF CYMBELINE

Once upon a time, walking was an essential part of everyday activity for most people. You walked to work, walked while you were working, walked for supplies, and eventually walked bearing your dead to the local church. If you were conscripted, it would often involve walking great distances, and sometimes from one end of the country to the other. Local village folk, harking back to a time when the country was made of small tribal kingdoms, often did not leave their local area in a lifetime. In other words, walking was a necessary function of everyday life, not something that you did, other than incidentally, for pleasure. Life was parochial and superstitious, controlled by Church and state, and there were few indications of what was going on in the centres of power. Travelling storytellers went from village to village to entertain the locals, often embroidering their tales to suit that particular area. It was in stark contrast to the way we live now with our metalled roads, first set up by the Romans; we think nothing of travel, and the place where you grew up is no longer of great importance.

Nowadays, there is a considerable emphasis on walking for pleasure, on walking to keep fit, and groups of ramblers roam the country on extended days out. All very enjoyable and very necessary in a country which is jammed to the gills, due as much to immigration as it is to the inherent population growth. We need to walk to breathe, to get away from other people and, unconsciously perhaps, to connect with the things that really matter in life. That was one of the apparent aims used in the promotion of Metro-land, although it was not a particularly original idea. On the contrary it was rather belated, because the construction of the railways in the 19th century often went hand in hand with the promotion of the areas they cut through, sometimes to the horror of the large landowners, who saw their power base threatened. For just as the coming of the railways created new communities, it also sometimes broke up established ones.

The Victorian era was a time of massive industrial change, but it also sparked the beginning of a new leisure industry, anything from messing about in boats on the Thames to walking in the country. So while there was nothing new in the steady stream of Met Line leaflets promoting the joys of country exploration, it did also kickstart the idea of getting out at the weekend, starting with a train trip to a chosen rural area. For the men behind the building of the Metropolitan Line, it was a win-win situation, with commuters during the week and leisure travelling at the weekend.

So let us turn our attention to the Chilterns in the Buckinghamshire countryside and remember a day out 50 years ago. It was a curious Sunday. Armed with my wife and both of my parents-in-law, we made a journey into the Chilterns while the latter were still reasonably fit. We were near Cadsden, which frequently figures in *Midsomer Murders*. After leaving the car, my father-in-law and I opted to separate from my wife and her mother to make the more accessible journey across the fields towards Ellesborough while we undertook a rather more difficult climb on the other side of the road, into the dense trees that formed the backdrop to the open meadows. It was steeper and more slippery than anticipated and I feared for my father-in-law on such a steep slope, no longer in the first flush of middle age. His daily cigarette intake didn't help, roughly equivalent to his age. But he braved it stoically, looking forward to a drink at The Plough afterwards.

It was in these same woods, the density of which preclude many visitors that, on another occasion, I found an Iron Age hill fort hidden high up amongst the trees. It had few visitors and a strange atmosphere, disturbed only by the rustling of the wind, but was clearly the keeper of many ancient tales from long ago. While glad to have discovered it, I felt uneasy being there, as if disturbing the brooding nature of the place. I had wandered into an area in which I could play no part because I was out of that time, an unwanted intruder trying to uncover long-hidden secrets. It would have made a good story for M. R. James.

Having achieved the heights, we spotted our other halves, Lowry-like in the distant fields, and determined to join them. But before we could do so, they had had their own strange experience. Apparently they had run into a middle-aged couple who had asked whether my wife and her mother had recently passed a girl heading in the opposite direction. "Why, no", they said, puzzled. "Absolutely nobody." The other couple looked troubled. Apparently they had seen their daughter running across the fields and could not understand why she was there rather than at home, and why she had not acknowledged them. She was supposed to have remained in Harrow and they couldn't understand why she should be in Buckinghamshire, or even how she could have got there. By rights she should have passed my wife and her mother but they had seen nobody, not even at a distance. Was it a portent of something else? We never found out. Another tale for M. R. James.

A mile or two further on, there is the splendid ancient church at Ellesborough, a favourite of Mrs Thatcher, who prayed there during the Falklands War. The church of Saints Peter and Paul, originally Catholic, stands atop a hill overlooking the village. The central and original part of the building dates from the 15th century, though further extensions were added in the 19th century. The church contains memorials to Sir Robert Croke and his family, an MP from the 17th century (Wikipedia, 2024). You might think we are a little off course for Metro-land, but no. Nearby is the single-track branch line that runs from Princes Risborough to Aylesbury, which was part of the Met in the 19th century.

Ellesborough is the starting point for the most wonderful walk which skirts Beacon Hill; it is actually part of the Icknield Way, an ancient trackway from the Neolithic Age which ran all the way from Avebury to Norfolk. Apart from the nearby prime minister's country abode, Chequers, the walk features the splendid site of Cymbeline's castle, set on the hillside with a splendid view of Aylesbury Vale. Featuring in Shakespeare's play, it actually refers to the British king and tribal leader Cunobelinus, who is said to have fought invasion by the Romans. He appears to have been part of the local tribe from whence we derive the name Chiltern. The actual fortification was once a motte and bailey castle from where the king would have had a panoramic view of incoming marauders. It seems a relatively insignificant spot these days, and one which is no doubt easily missed by those not in the know. Disappointingly few people take account of our ancient history, yet the clues are everywhere. Our eyes are more easily distracted by the top of Beacon Hill and its lonely tree. The views do not compete with the highest point in the Chilterns, nearby Coombe Hill, but it is less busy, allowing more time for contemplation. It was a walk I did regularly whenever I wanted to blow away the problems of the time and, like a coastal walk, it never disappoints, and it is easy to understand the pleasures of Chequers, away from the bustle of Downing Street.

Chequers, approximately 40 miles from Downing Street, is the country house of the serving UK prime minister. It is close to both Ellesborough and Wendover, at the foot of the Chiltern Hills. Coombe Hill is less than a mile away. However, it has only been the PM's bolthole for about a hundred years since the house was given to the nation by Arthur Lee,

1st Viscount Lee, probably in exchange for his title. He had been there for 12 years, 1909–1921. It is Grade 1 listed and dates from about 1565, when it was built by William Hawtrey.

> The name "Chequers" may derive from an early owner of the manor of Ellesborough in the 12th century, Elias Ostiarius (or de Scaccario). The name "Ostiarius" meant an usher of the court of Exchequer, and *scacchiera* means a chessboard in Italian. Elias Ostiarius's coat of arms included the chequer board of the Exchequer, so the estate may be named after his arms and position at court. (Wikipedia, 2025)

Historian David Starkey, in his book *Elizabeth: Apprenticeship* (2001), offers an alternative view; that the chequer trees growing in the grounds were responsible for the name. I think it more likely that the trees were planted there to match the origin of the estate and to provide a sense of uniformity.

Lady Mary Grey, younger sister of Lady Jane Grey and great-granddaughter of Henry VII, was confined at Chequers for two years as punishment for marrying without the monarch's consent. She was banished from court and confined there from 1565–1567.

Chequers passed through a number of different families as a result of descent through the female line, among them the Wooleys, Crokes and Thurbanes. There is also a strong connection to the Cromwell family because, in 1715, the female owner of the house married John Russell, a grandson of Oliver Cromwell. The house contains a collection of Cromwell memorabilia. I am grateful to Wikipedia 2025 for all the above information.

> In the 19th century, the Russells (by now the Greenhill-Russell family) employed Henry Rhodes to make alterations to the house in the Gothic style. The Tudor panelling and windows were ripped out, and battlements and pinnacles installed. Towards the end of the 19th century, the house passed through marriage to the Astley family. Between 1892 and 1901, Bernard Astley restored the house to its Elizabethan origins, with advice from Reginald Blomfeld. The restoration and design work was completed by John Birch, architect. (Wikipedia, 2025)

By now you may be thinking that outer Metro-land is simply a place for toffs but, compared with the total land area utilised by the Met in its development north-west of London, it either simply overlaid what was there – or even not there – previously and, of course, was compelled to fit in with history. However, your average Metro man was conceived as a working commuter, even if the larger villas along the route were occupied by company directors rather than drones. But what these special houses – like Chequers and the mansion at Moor Park – did, was to give a certain *cachet* to the area which made it that much more attractive as a place to live. They were the jewels in the crown certainly but their sparkle attracted others. Did I feel that much better for growing up next to the wealth of Moor Park even though I did not share it? Yes, I think I probably did.

The rest of the walk is a pleasant trawl through Chiltern countryside. Yet, sadly, walking alone in the country has its risks these days, as England is no longer a safe place. While most killings are generally done by someone who knows the victim, others that take place, often in the country, are more random and born of opportunity rather than planning. So those that wander the country hills and dales, often with a dog but worse by themselves, are now taking a demonstrable risk. Not what the promoters of Metro-land had in mind at all. In their leaflets there is no sense of threat. So whether this has come about through population growth or immigration, or a vague jealousy about the good fortune of others, is hard to pin down. What is clear is that successive governments have done little or nothing to curb it. So safer perhaps to visit controlled country areas such as those run by the National Trust, English Heritage or Historic England, where there is usually someone around to keep an eye on you even if you don't agree with the more woke politics of the owner.

Moving on to Wendover, H. V. Borley recounts the following in an issue of *The Railway Magazine*.

> At a short distance from the railway station, the great slopes are covered by interminable stretches of wooden trellis and skeletons of wooden-framed houses. Some 20,000 troops are now in training. (1914)

The Met, still thinking commercially, encouraged the day-tripper to go and observe the troops being trained to fight in this bloodiest and muddiest of all wars. By contrast, and I was quite unaware of this, there was a branch line to Halton camp, which had been constructed in 1917 by German POWs.

The Burma railway it was not. Instead the prisoners were set to work felling beech trees, and the line (abandoned since 1963) was employed to take coal and other goods to the camp, which eventually became an RAF station. The Air Ministry supplied its own locomotives to haul the trains on this branch, which was nearly two miles long. There was also a passing loop that became disused some time before the branch itself closed. Careful detective work can reveal evidence of this little-known branch and I think it is possible that the line snaked through the car park at the rear of the Red Lion pub, an old coaching inn. The reason for my thinking this is that many years ago, the car park had an old railway gate at its exit; it would make sense for the line to have taken that route, since any further north the railway would have clashed with the town streets. So my conjecture is that it branched off what is now the Chiltern Line before reaching Wendover station, and cut across the Wendover/Amersham road to reach the aforementioned car park. Incidentally, *The Railway Magazine* is still in circulation after 125 years.

We can't leave Wendover without considering Coombe Hill, at 260 metres the highest point in the Chilterns. It is now managed by the National Trust and the view from the top is well worth the climb, giving a splendid outlook over Aylesbury Vale and much of the northern part of Metro-land. At the summit is a memorial to those who died in the Boer War, and the NT offer prescribed paths over the hill and close to Chequers. All very well you might say, but I cannot help but feel that the site, like so many others run by the NT, has now been sanitised for your convenience, complete with, of course, paying car park. Why is it we cannot be allowed to explore our countryside unfettered by the shackles of officialdom? I know there are plenty of free spaces, but even so.

Coombe Hill offers the chance to see the local wildlife and, in particular, the glorious Red Kite, only recently re-introduced, but now there are far too many. In my childhood there were none at all. Those headstrong re-wilders that carried out this unwise task may not have realised that in their attempts to encourage the bird, they have actually unbalanced nature in terms of what was already there, rather than the reverse. Not a good result when the Chilterns are now overrun with Red Kites that seem to breed like rabbits (pardon the mixed metaphor) at the expense of everything else.

Still, even this is preferable to the horror that is now Aylesbury, an old market town which has spread indiscriminately and is now almost joined to Wendover which, in turn, will soon be joined to Amersham, partly because of the building of HS2. The government and the local planners have ruined this very special part of the Chilterns. Building another railway underground, of no value to the locals and parallel to the excellent Chiltern Line, is an act of monumental folly both for the taxpayer and the splendid countryside that has now been destroyed in the process. Yet nobody takes responsibility for these acts of vandalism and, if they are ever found, it is my sincere hope that they will be eventually pecked to death by the aforementioned Red Kites.

Sadly the damage done by the construction of HS2 is not confined to this side of Aylesbury, and similar blotches across the countryside can be found way beyond, stretching into farthest Buckinghamshire. A crying shame as well as utterly pointless.

The Met, when it ran that far, had its own separate station at Aylesbury, Brook Street. But it was only open for two years (1892–94), when the Met was combined with the main station at Aylesbury. Brook Street reminds me of the long-forgotten secretarial agency, Brook Street Bureau, and that led me on to thinking about a short-lived underground advertisement for Speedwriting, a sort of fast-track approach for those who couldn't type or perhaps even spell. "Gt a gd jb and mo pa." Perhaps I should have adopted Speedwriting for this book. Thn it wd hv bn a lt shrtr.

In December 1904, there was a terrible accident at Aylesbury station when a fast GC newspaper train (in thick fog) failed to brake for the then maximum 15mph curve just south of the station, resulting in total derailment and the deaths of several people, including the driver and fireman. Coaches mounted both the up and down platforms. and part of the train was smashed to bits. A train travelling in the opposite direction was fortunately able to slam on the brakes and come to a halt before reaching the wreckage, which was strewn everywhere. There was some doubt as to how well the driver knew the line but, having travelled it in a similarly thick fog at speed when signalling was hugely inferior to today, I feel lucky to have survived. As a result of this accident the offending curve was redesigned in 1908 to make it less extreme, as newspaper trains, not stopping at Aylesbury, were known for their high speeds. It is axiomatic that more speed means less safety and so when accidents do occasionally occur on today's high-speed lines, the results tend to be more devastating.

While I don't have a great deal of time for Aylesbury, I suppose I should declare that large conurbations, bent on commercialism, generally carry little appeal to me. However, within the nearby surrounds there are a few gems. One of these is Hartwell House, to be found just off the A418 heading for Thame to the west of the town.

Hartwell House is a fine Grade I listed Jacobean mansion which has been a hotel since 1989. It is owned by the Ernest Cook Trust and has been leased to the National Trust. It is only 3 miles from the centre of Aylesbury, but behind its protective wall, it is a world away from the seething masses and, fortunately, some 40 miles from London. Its history goes back as far as the Domesday Book of 1086, when the original building was owned by William Peverel.

The present house owes its existence to the Hampden family, the Lee family acquiring it through marriage with the Hampdens in 1650. It has European connections, as described by Wikipedia.

> Between 1809 and 1814 the owner of the house, Sir Charles Lee, let the mansion to the French prince Louis Stanislas Xavier, Count of Provence, the future King Louis XVIII. The arrival of the impoverished prince and his court at Hartwell was not a happy experience for the mansion, with once grand and imperious courtiers farming chickens and assorted small livestock on the lead roofs. (2025)

Where you might have imagined a scene from Dumas set in Buckinghamshire, what you actually got was more of a grand country commune.

> Louis's wife, Marie Josephine of Savoy, died at Hartwell in 1810. After her death, her body was carried first to Westminster Abbey, and later to Sardinia, where the Savoy king had withdrawn during [the] Napoleonic invasion of Turin and Piedmont; she is buried in Cagliari Cathedral. Prince Louis signed the document accepting the French crown in the library of the house, following the defeat of Napoleon. (2025)

In another strange aspect of its history, Dr John Lee inherited the house in 1827 and, as a result of this, formed the British (now Royal) Meteorological Society in 1850. A friendly scientist, William Henry Smyth, helped with the design of the telescope and cupola that Lee installed. From this the Hartwell Observatory was born.

Following the death of the Lees, the house remained a private residence until 1938 when, in danger of demolition, it was acquired by philanthropist Ernest Cook who auctioned off most of the contents. In the 1960s it became a girls' finishing school, and in the late 1980s it was let to the Historic Hotel Group. Being very close to Chequers at Wendover, it has often served as a suitable venue for government meetings and international summits, accompanied by a fine cuisine often featuring Aylesbury duck. Though why anyone would want a duck from Aylesbury, I cannot imagine. Wikipedia advises that

> Between 1759 and 1761, architect Henry Keene substantially enlarged and "Georgianised" the house, and built the east front with its canted bay windows and a central porch in the Tuscan style. Inside, the great hall has stucco panels, and three reception rooms with rococo chimneypieces.
>
> The 1980s conversion to a hotel was overseen by the architect Eric Throssell who created a new dining room in the style of Sir John Soane, by enclosing the former 18th-century open arcaded porch. The former semi-circular galleried entrance vestibule became an inner hall. Throssell was also responsible for the design and recreation of the cupola crowning the roof. (2025)

It seems a shame that this Jacobean manor house was Georgianised, since there are so few of the former and a goodly supply of the latter. There are also 90 acres of gardens designed by Capability Brown in around 1750, which draw comparison with Stowe in terms of their statues, obelisk and ornamental bridge. The entire estate covers 1,800 acres, although ever threatened by the proximity of Aylesbury and its new build.

Many years ago we used to live a few miles along the road from Hartwell House in a pretty little village where the local councillor refused to believe that the very modest front lawn in front of our house belonged to us, despite the protestations of our solicitor, and where a dog called Sally, three doors down and improperly attended, frequently delivered pancakes of the non-Shrove Tuesday variety to our garden.

The joys of an English village were further promoted when one day we found a family parked up in our drive. When asked what they were doing they claimed the previous owner had always given them permission to park there to attend a local annual event. It took some time to disabuse them that that permission no longer existed, if indeed it had ever done in the first place.

Next door lived a very fierce Alsatian, improperly controlled by a frequently drunken housewife. One day our normally placid collie acted quite out of character against this animal when, sensing it was not well, it launched a guerilla attack from the garage roof. Fortunately the fight was stopped before it got out of control.

The usual attempt to billet several dozen new houses just up the hill was resisted but, no doubt, not for long. I also remember the two coldest nights of any winter that I have experienced in the UK, at −17°C. Another incomer hooked himself up to the local water supply without permission from the local water board. I am not sure if it was ever resolved.

It was not all bad. Occasional visits to the local manor house were pleasant enough but it made me realise how so many are never satisfied with what they have got and push over the boundaries of what is acceptable, spoiling other people's lives in the process. That situation is far worse now than it ever was and the very antithesis of what Metro-land was designed for. Money speaks and its voice is not always a pleasant one.

Another NT site, Waddesdon Manor, lies out beyond Aylesbury and was recently occupied by the Rothschilds, one of Europe's wealthiest families. The Buckinghamshire County Museum tells us about its construction.

> Building materials and fully-grown trees were transported to the summit of Lodge Hill, upon which the manor was constructed in the 1870s. (104, 1986)

It is one of the youngest of the great houses that I have considered in this volume.

> The Wotton Tramway, as the Brill branch was then known, had been opened only a year or so previously [in the 1890s] and was used to bring the materials to the foot of the hill from a spur at Wotton Station. Telegraph wires had to be lowered to allow the extraordinary loads to be moved. Teams of Percheron mares from Normandy were employed to haul the loads from the terminus of the special branch. (104, 1986)

The Waddesdon website, proudly proclaiming "A Rothschild house and gardens", describes its origins.

> Baron Ferdinand [de Rothschild] wanted an estate where he could escape London in the summer months to entertain family and friends for weekend house parties. The Vale of Aylesbury was already known as "Rothschildshire" for the number of houses owned by the family in the area.
>
> When he came into his inheritance in 1874 he purchased a bare agricultural estate with a misshapen cone at its centre. The foundation stone was laid in 1877 and six years later the land had been transformed

> into a beautiful landscape by planting mature trees, bringing in the water supply from Aylesbury and removing 30 feet of soil to create the impressive approach to the house. (2025)

The house was designed to be in the style of the French Renaissance châteaux which can be found in the Loire valley, with which I am quite familiar. The only notable differences between going round one of the French châteaux and Waddesdon is the fact that the National Trust do at least serve refreshments to the visitor, but unfortunately the location of Waddesdon ensures that it does not usually have the same balmy French weather to go with it. But it did have a French architect: Gabriel-Hyppolyte Destailleur. Sounds more like a whiskey manufacturer. Whilst he did not want to construct a palace, Ferdinand had a wing added to the west end of the house which increased its footprint by nearly 50 per cent.

After ten years in construction, the house was completed by 1883, celebrated by a series of house parties. The house was ahead of its time in many respects.

> Running water and central heating were provided from the start and electricity was introduced in 1889. Ferdinand put in a small passenger lift for Queen Victoria's visit in 1890… but she declined to ride in it, not trusting the magic of electricity. (2025)

One is immediately struck, when considering these great houses, by the chasm of difference at this time between the very rich and the poor, confined to abysmal slum conditions. You can argue that such a chasm exists today, although what one sees now is the triviality of so many of them, like the Beckhams. Also, it seems that the presence of money, rather than providing comfort, is often the source of bitter wrangling, either because of divorce or inheritance and a perceived entitlement to a share of it.

Waddesdon seems a good example of extreme wealth, carefully and privately conserved by the Rothschild family behind closed doors. We are told that conditions remained much the same until the Second World War, when 100 evacuee children were given a temporary home there.

After the war James de Rothschild was said to be extremely anxious about the future of Waddesdon, this in an era of high taxation, especially upon the death of the owner of a country pile.

> He decided to bequeath Waddesdon to the National Trust, with a large part of the collections and an area of garden. The Trust was not

> complimentary about the architecture, but considered the collections as superlative. (2025)

It seems a little odd that the Trust were so sniffy about the building and one can only assume that they considered it (rather parochially perhaps) as too non-English and, in its attempts to resemble a Renaissance château, too exotic. However, they were not completely put off since James R also left the largest endowment the Trust had ever received to ensure upkeep of the property. In fact it remains the only example of the famous "Rothschild style" of the 19th century that was open to the public.

> His widow, Dorothy, oversaw the opening of the house to the public in 1959 and chaired the management committee until her death in 1988. (2025)

She had begun a survey into the condition of the roof which Jacob, 4th Lord Rothschild and her heir, expanded into a full-blown renovation of the house and everything in it. Consequently the house was closed and emptied of its possessions in 1990 to allow this, only partially reopening some five years later.

> During this time the Wine Cellars were created, the dilapidated Dairy was rebuilt, and the formal planting of the Parterre was restored to its extravagant 19th century appearance. (2025)

Royalty lent its favours to Waddesdon on several occasions. Queen Victoria visited Waddesdon Manor on 14 May 1890, and was carried round the estate in a bath-chair drawn by a pony. There is, I understand, some early film of the event. Edward VII visited the house on a number of occasions, drawn by its numerous attractions. He arrived by train on the Metropolitan Line, alighting from Waddesdon Manor station which had been specially built for the family. There can scarcely have been a better way to promote the Met than for it to receive royal patronage. In so doing it formed the finest possible reason to set up home in Metro-land for generations to come. At this point in the 21st century, it may be difficult for us to understand the positivity behind the building of the Met, jaded as we are now in a country apparently in the process of a long decline.

In reading through the history of this property I think I spotted the subtlest of criticisms of the Rothschilds by the National Trust, as if the family should have done a little more for the community. But then anyone who is familiar with the recent history of the NT will know that they have done little to endear themselves to certain sections of the membership by an increasingly woke approach to their work, rather than adhering to their relatively simple brief of obtaining and preserving the finest of our properties and gardens for the future. I have no doubt that there are many within the army of volunteers who do such splendid unpaid work who do not feel like this, but a certain antagonism has grown up in recent years between the NT and its supporters that should not be present, resulting in a loss of membership and a resultantly poor press.

It is a curse of the age that in so many areas of business these days, we have allowed ourselves to become distracted with irrelevancies such as apologising for our involvement in history (unavoidable) and in the slave trade (far too late). This has coloured the thinking of certain NT employees in their presentation of events within particular properties, instead of accepting that we cannot alter history by simply apologising for it or trying to retrospectively alter the facts. Once started on this path there are endless things that we would not tolerate now, such as the exploitation of children in the mills and mines and the treatment of women as second-class citizens. The job of the NT is to record history to encourage an understanding of the past rather than to alter the emphasis of its exhibits as if such problems never existed, reflecting only today's attitudes. This in tandem with a rather woke mentality has gotten the NT into the problems in which it now finds itself and is currently unable to resolve.

The NT is by no means alone in this, and one could name a number of household names that have allowed themselves to drift from their remit. This lack of focus may be why, in terms of management, the country is drifting dangerously towards incompetence and a lack of cohesion. Our politicians today completely lack the visionary attitudes of the Victorians and show no real concern for the country, replaced with a desire to promote themselves and a failure to understand how supposedly idealistic Marxist policies of the past can lead to chaos and poverty.

What sort of regulator is it that allows water bills to rise by 25 per cent while sewage is still disgracefully expelled into our rivers? Such increases, besides putting a strain on the private purse, can lead the poorer members of society into poverty, since their wages don't have a hope of matching the ever-increasing taxation that is thrust upon the community, coupled with a lack of realisation that such increases never mean more money for the Exchequer, but instead more people who cannot pay and a resultant increase in benefits. This is illustrated in tax freedom day, which measures the effect of taxes in any one financial year before one can keep a portion of what you actually earn. Not unnaturally, it is becoming later with each passing year, and it may soon cease to exist at all as we become slaves to the government machine. Again, I digress.

However, since this volume is about railways, it is worth mentioning that despite other incompetent politicians, Michael Portillo's excellent and continuing series of *Great British Railway Journeys* is able to put a very positive spin on life in this country today by emphasising the skills of local craftsmen and farmers as he travels around the country. Whether it is enthusiasts restoring old steam locomotives or preserving unusual species of trees, there is an inner heart to this country that still refreshingly teaches old crafts to young people or helps develop new ones. For the younger generation, despite the mindless threshing of a line of weak politicians, still helps preserve the past and creates a positive future against the hideous background of largely unfettered crime.

At this point we are now some 40 miles away from the centre of London, and the tone of the area has changed from close-knit houses backing on to the railway to the fresher smell of the country. Bill Bryson (2015), on the other hand, thought that Portillo only got off the train to spend about forty seconds talking about something that was no longer there. A little unfair perhaps but quite funny. Yet, while this was true in the development of the railway and in my childhood, it now seems dangerously threatened. I used to have a dream as a child that portrayed England as totally concreted over, a nightmarish hardstanding when there were no trees, no wildlife and only bisecting roads. Although they stretched as far as the eye could see, they seemed merely roads to nowhere, because everything was the same and this country, which was once entirely wooded (the Romans even described parts of the south as jungle), was now entirely concrete and, as a result, totally soulless. You could not walk more than a few yards for fear of being run over. Sometimes, that same feeling of hopelessness recurs as I travel along motorways in the pouring rain. What have we done to our planet?

I like to think that if they were brought back to assess the progress that they themselves had begun, the visionaries of Metro-land would be appalled, and would claim it had all gone too far. Yet there are still faint hopes for the future in the announcement of an increase in national forests and the rewilding of certain areas. There is even a sanctuary on the Weald where you can familiarise yourself with all our major indigenous wildlife, including a large owl who goes by the name of Ethel. It is an excellent educational tool and reminds me how H. G. Wells, a teacher before he became famous, took A. A. Milne and other boys from the school on regular outings to learn about the countryside. As we know, it stayed with Milne all his life, resulting in the Hundred Acre Wood (actually a section of Ashdown Forest), with the fictional Christopher Robin acting as a guide, not the real one.

This is remarkably close in tone to some of the Met's leaflets extolling the countryside, and portraying an imaginary past as completely unthreatening and desirable, as in any of Milne's books. Of course, real life is not like that, but in so far as the Met's authors were concerned, it was necessary to create a rural perfection that everyone could aspire to. In this respect it was not much different to any other advertisement for a product, except that in the Met's case it was much wider and all encompassing, suggesting a template for a life.

> This is a good parcel of English soil in which to build a home and take root. (6, 1986)

The trouble is if everyone does it, the attraction wains and the law of diminishing returns sets in, and I think that's probably where we have got to.

Along the Brill branch of the Met, originally just a tramway, close to remote Wotton, lay, quite extraordinarily, a second Wotton station. This one was barely 200 yards away from the Met station in what can only be described as a country backwater. Edwards and Pilgram utilise Annie Kirby to explain why.

> The Great Central Railway between Calvert and the GWR at Ashendon Junction was built following a long argument between the two companies which reached a climax on 30 July 1898. The Met's Chairman, John Bell, had heard that his former office colleague William Pollitt (who had become General Manager of the GCR) proposed to run trains from the north of England on to the GWR line at Aylesbury, so by-passing the Met's main line south to Harrow, which was leased to the Great Central. Bell personally set the signals against this train. This event resulted in the Great Central concluding an agreement with the Great Western for a new route to London via Princes Risborough and High Wycombe. (109, 1986)

This dispute was eventually forgotten when the stationmaster for the GCR also looked after the Met station at Wotton. To have two such stations in such a remote country spot was extremely peculiar and, unsurprisingly, most of the rail traffic used the faster and more direct GCR route rather than the bumpy, oil-lit Brill branch to Quainton Road. Just to confirm itself as the winner the GCR, which began operations in 1906, advertised itself as "the Line of Health", a sly dig at the more exotically worded leaflets put out by the Met at that time.

Also at Wotton Underwood was a long-vanished Kingswood branch, of which almost nothing is known apart from the fact that it was abandoned before the First World War. Old maps show a number of these minor branches, which saw limited use and went out of service while the infamous Dr Beeching was still in short trousers. Many were put in place to serve minor industries of the time such as the old tile works, and were not in any sense part of the commercial running of the Met. But they were part of the local landscape in their preservation of old trades.

Buckinghamshire County Museum tells us that there used to be two old windmills on the hill at Brill, the 1680 original falling victim to a storm on one of the highest areas of the Chilterns. It can be seen in old prints. The surviving windmill (c. 1757), often included in Metro-land literature, is typical of the Met's determination to be associated with a dreamy past, despite, at the same time, the promotion of a modern railway for the north-west suburbs. Of course, Brill was never on the main line and, for most people considering a home suitable for commuting, it was both too far out of town and at the end of a rickety branch line. Nevertheless, despite its impracticality, it was good for advertising.

Edwards and Pilgram tell us that

> The building of the Great Central Railway across the green south Midlands to London was an important event – the last mainline railway to be made in Britain. The Manchester, Sheffield & Lincolnshire Railway's Bill received Royal Assent in 1893 and work began on the 92 miles of new line from Nottingham to Quainton Road. The first coal train ran through to Marylebone on 25 July 1898 and the first passenger trains began on 15 March 1899. (122, 1986)

Yet the GC was only open for 67 years, a remarkably short time for a main line. I remember its closure, which seemed a dreadful mistake at the time and, in the light of HS2, an even bigger one now. I mention all this because of the close connection between the Great Central and the

Met for part of its route. However, it seems to have finally dawned on our politicians that railways are a relatively cheap and efficient way to move people around: when, and I make the point strongly, they have been properly thought out in the first place. As a result, a number of old routes are coming back to life again like the Oxford and Cambridge link, where that route has not been permanently destroyed by new building and roads.

In a few cases, they are assisted by the enthusiastic volunteers of heritage lines, where a connection would be useful to both parties. I am all in favour of this, although the Met is unlikely to change a great deal, having discovered its permanent way after a good deal of wriggling in the early years. An extra station has however been added to the Chiltern Line, beyond Aylesbury at Aylesbury Vale Parkway on the old GC route, because of the expansion of the town.

Driving through the area north of Aylesbury today, it is fascinating to find evidence of the old stations along the GC route. I cannot be alone in thinking this because of the formation of the Buckinghamshire Railway Museum at Quainton Road. I am, of course, mentioning these outlying areas because they were, for a while, part of the Met route to Verney Junction, once its most outlying station. But it only went that far because of the personal requirements of the local landowners; it was probably a pretty daft idea because it could never pay its way with such a sparse local population. However, it does show the clout that these old-style aristocrats once had, now faded away by virtue of those two certainties, death and taxes. They even had their own private halts for family use only.

MORE RECENTLY

London Transport has been through a number of changes of ownership, currently as part of Transport for London, but the Metropolitan Line continues to run as a separate management unit within the overall structure.

There was a need to replace some of the signalling, a great deal of which dated to before the Second World War. Mike Horne tells us that

> In 1974 London Transport made an early foray into computerised signalling when a minicomputer was installed at Watford, where it temporarily took over control from the programme machines until it was moved to Heathrow Central. The computer, minute by modern standards, proved quite robust and started more serious development work on computer controlled signalling. (91, 2003)

I remember that the London end of the parallel old Great Central (now Chiltern Line) had old-style semaphore signalling very late in the section leading up to Harrow-on-the-Hill. It was rather terrifying to be hurtling through the fog, knowing that the only thing between you and oblivion was an obscure semaphore signal.

Remarkably, the Baker Street signal box, in use for at least 60 years, was not modernised until 1987, replaced by a new interlocking device. In addition, the ticketing system has been completely modernised so that you can travel by just swiping your card.

Over the years, management has tried various schemes to improve reliability by fiddling with the number of stations that each train should stop at, the main losers being the Watford and Uxbridge branches reverting to all stations stopping. Now the Met operates on a simplified clockface principle, except during peak hours in combination with the Chiltern Line out of Marylebone. At one time half-length trains were run on the Met during off-peak hours, but this was abandoned after the inconvenience of coupling and uncoupling rolling stock was taken into account, especially in poor weather conditions. Mostly unknown to the public, train-running has been affected by such things as staff shortages, acute at one time, and the merging point south of Wembley Park of the slow and fast lines.

I remember that the homecoming Met train would sometimes cross tracks to the outer Chiltern Line platform at Harrow-on-the-Hill in preparation for running fast to Moor Park, though that was by no means mandatory. Despite this, speed limits have been reduced at times, possibly because of the uncomfortably bumpy and swaying ride on elderly rolling stock.

It is a curious fact that Chiltern Line trains, when travelling on shared Metropolitan Line tracks (between Amersham and Harrow) are subject to London Underground signalling rules, whereas the rest of the time they are subject to Network Rail procedures. As a result cabs have been modified to cope with both. A simple example is the W (for whistle) used on signs in Network Rail areas, which is otherwise replaced by WHISTLE on the Met.

Despite all the aforementioned, the Met remains an important and prestigious line of which Edward Watkin would have been proud, despite its contraction in length. Of course, it would be foolish to think that there will be no further changes to the Met. The wrong-headed Dr Beeching has shown in his wanton destruction of perfectly good lines, along with the bad, that he was just storing up problems for the future through a bludgeoning short-termism, just like so many of our politicians.

For the moment though, the Met seems to have reached a comfortable plateau, and the railway jigsaw, that initially did not quite fit together, has been re-assembled and Metro-land seems complete.

> Much has changed in Metro-land in the post war period. Just as Metro-land had itself swallowed up tiny villages, the ever growing metropolis submerged the Arcadian ideal sold in those posters from the MCRE. Now the former villages and Garden suburbs of Wembley, Pinner and Harrow have become part of the endless sprawl of London, losing some of their unique character. (*Modernism in Metro-Land*, 2025)

CONCLUSIONS

So what are we to make of Metro-land today and where does it sit in relation to the development of the country's railways? I have mixed feelings about it but I am more in favour of it than against. No western European country can stand still if it wants to maintain its place in the world, and we have much for which to thank the Victorian visionaries who initially conceived the idea of an underground railway, which eventually spread as far from London as could be imagined, into the middle of Buckinghamshire. In fact, it really is a misnomer to call it an underground railway at all, since in excess of 90 per cent of the route is overground. This, in turn, begs the question as to whether the rolling stock in some way inhibits the value of the line, because it was obviously designed for mainly underground use and shortish journeys outside that. The problem is that one of the main drivers of the scheme (no pun intended) was to breathe new life into a stagnating City, and this could only be achieved with the appropriate underground stock. So while the outer limits beg for something better, the two ends of the line are irreconcilable from this point of view.

Pushing forward the railway from its humble beginnings as a short steam-driven line in central London to a place some 50 miles from the capital (in a relatively short space of time, which in itself was interrupted by world war) is really quite exceptional. In particular, we have to thank Sir Edward Watkin for his remarkable foresight and determination. The concept of acquiring enough land alongside the route to build housing on an industrial scale was ingenious; in so doing, the line was ensuring a large passenger base that would justify its future existence. Of course, this came at a tremendous cost: the destruction of large swathes of countryside which, strangely, the leaflets advertising Metro-land seemed inordinately keen to promote. I was aware of this as a child, and despite the creation of many relatively soulless suburbs along the route, I was lucky enough to be living on the edge of the country and so was relatively unaffected. The Wembley exhibition of a hundred years ago did much to

137

promote the route, even if its primary purpose as a celebration of Empire was, even then, woefully out of date. More like a wake.

The Met also did its bit for the war effort by growing crops in the hitherto undeveloped fields along the route to help both its own railwaymen and others. By the time I was growing up in the latter part of the 20th century, we were saying a final goodbye to the ration books and were living relatively comfortably. I think it was an ingenious idea to create some sense of individuality in many of the modest houses in the garden villages along the route, and although they might seem slightly twee today (e.g. a small piece of stained-glass design in the front door), we should remember that, at that time, the rampant commercialism that we know today had not started, and we were relatively happy with what we had. Life was simpler and there was no sense then that we should acquire more and more to be successful.

So although, as a child, I never really quantified the idea of Metro-land, there is no doubt that I enjoyed what it provided me with, together with the opportunity to explore the nearby countryside. The history of this country is often hidden in its old buildings and their surrounds. There are many of those in Metro-land to be enjoyed, as well as its fields and woodland. I am horrified what the HS2 works have done to the Chilterns: untold damage to the countryside when there is a perfectly serviceable railway nearby. Yet this great project, originally intended to have covered many miles with branches to the north-west and north-east, has now been scaled back to simply London to Birmingham, a route that is already well covered by other lines, the original of which took just five years to build. In the many years that HS2 has been in the offing, there has been an enormous amount of huffing but very little actual puffing, and untold damage to the environment. Ultimately, we might just end up with a result so puny we will be laughed at by our neighbours on the continent. In fact we probably already are.

What is more, in the age of screens, such travel will be rendered largely out of date. Why travel when a good-quality video conference is there at the touch of a button? Perhaps, in the future, there will be visitor centres to gawp at the folly of successive governments who were unable to manage the project, wasting ever-increasing billions of tax payers' money in the process. In so doing, the glory of Metro-land is now gradually fading and the sun setting on the lark-abundant (!) fields. Metro-land was created by one railway, destroyed by another. It seems the ultimate irony.

My hope is, if you have enjoyed this book, that you will go in Search of your own favourite piece of Metro-land. While I have concentrated partly on the country houses in the area, the real secret treasure of Metro-land is in that area of special countryside, or particular building, that has an inner appeal to you personally and to which you return again and again in search of an inner peace. For me that would be on the hillside above Ellesborough, despite the Red Kites. It provides a superb example of being able to relate the present to our past history, something that we, in our headlong rush through life, tend to easily forget.

Evelyn Waugh, in his 1928 novel *Decline and Fall*, introduced a character called Viscount Metroland, who appears in two other of his novels and marries society lady Margot Beste-Chetwynd. Presumably Metro-land, the phrase originally coined in 1915, was his personal estate, which would probably make it larger than anything held by royalty, and stretch for a total distance of some 40 miles. If we compare it with the 13-mile length of the Sandringham Estate, we can appreciate the size of it. A nice conceit indeed.

ACKNOWLEDGEMENTS

My sincere thanks to Lord Ian Strathcarron and Lucy Duckworth and team for their help in the production of this book and in particular the brilliant cover design. Also to Madeleine and Keith Fletcher for their memories of life close to the Metropolitan Line and their assistance with a choice of reference books.

I am also extremely grateful for the assistance of Dennis Edwards and Ron Pilgram in terms of their books on Metro-land and their obvious love of the area. Sadly, what they celebrated is being gradually eroded because of HS2 and its lack of respect for the Chiltern Hills.

In any wide-ranging account such as this, the possibility of mistakes is considerable. As the author I take responsibility for these and undertake to make corrections in any future editions of this book. I hope they in no way obscure what was an important part of my young life.

BIBLIOGRAPHY AND FILMOGRAPHY

Amersham Society, *History of Old Amersham*, https://AmershamSociety.org, 31/01/25.
Anon, *Ace Cinema*, https:/en.wikipedia.org/wiki/Ace_Cinema, 12/03/25.
Anon, *Chenies – a brief history of the Village*, https://cheniesvillage.co.uk/village-history (1987), 23/03/25.
Anon, *Chesham*, https://en.wikipedia.org/wiki/Chesham, 13/02/25.
Anon, *Chequers*, https://en.wikipedia.org/wiki/chequers, 13/02/25.
Anon, *RAF Coastal Command*, https:en.wikipedia.org/wiki/RAF_Coastal_Command, 15/04/25.
Anon, *Edward Watkin*, https://en.wikipedia.org/wiki/Edward_Watkin, 27/02/25.
Anon, *Ellesborough Church*, https://en.wikipedia.org/wiki/Ellesborough, 08/01/24.
Anon, *Harrow on the Hill*, https://en.wikipedia.org/wiki/Harrow_on_the_Hill, 03/03/25.
Anon, *Harrow School*, https://en.wikipedia.org/wiki/Harrow_School, 20/03/25.
Anon, *Hartwell House, Buckinghamshire*, https://en.wikipedia.org/wiki/Hartwell_House,_Buckinghamshire, 06/05/25.
Anon, *History of Cliveden*, https://www.nationaltrust.org.uk/visit/oxfordshire-buckinghamshire-berkshire/cliveden/history-of-cliveden, 22/02/25.
Anon, *Merchant Taylors' Preparatory School*, https: //mtpn.org.uk/about-us/history, 05/04/25.
Anon, *Metro-land*, https://en.wikipedia.org/wiki/Metro-land, 22/12/24.
Anon, *Modernism in Metro-Land*, https//www. modernism_in_metroland.co.uk/metro-land and modernism.html, 12/06/25.
Anon, *Latimer House*, https://en.wikipedia.org/Latimer House, 25/01/25.
Anon, *Liberty Tomb*, https: //Liberty Tomb/cheniesvillage, 28/01/25.
Anon, *London 1948 Olympic Games*, https://www.Brittanica.com/event/London-Olympic-Games-1948, 02/05/2025.
Anon, *Metropolitan line*, https://en.wikipedia.org/Metropolitan_line, 03/12/24.
Anon, *Moor Park Mansion*, https:www.moorparkdflas.com/about-moor-park, 19/01/25.
Anon, *Pinner: a brief profile and history*, https://harrowonline.org/2022/08/24/history-of-pinner-in-harrow/#google_vignette, 04/03/25.
Anon, *Rickmansworth*, https: //en.wikipedia.org/Rickmansworth, 02/02/25.

Anon, *Shardeloes*, https://en.wikipedia.org/shardeloes, 14/02/25.
Anon, *Waddesdon – History*, https://waddesdon.org.uk, 17/04/25.
Ayshford D., *Chenies*, https://cheniesvillage.co.uk/village-history, 23/03/25.
Bilyeau N., *Medmenham Abbey – Home of the Notorious Secret Society 'Hellfire Club'*, https://www.thevintagenews.com/2018-05-11/medmenhamabbey, 20/02/25.
Betjeman J., *Metro-Land*, d. Edward Mirzoeff, BBC, London, UK, 1972.
Borley H. V., *The Railway Magazine*, Mortons Media Group Ltd, Horncastle, Autumn 1914.
Bryson B., The Road to Little Dribbling, London, Penguin Random House, 2015.
Conrad J., *Heart of Darkness*, London, 1899.
Engel M., *Eleven Minutes Late: A Train Journey into the Soul of Britain*, Pan MacMillan, Basingstoke and Oxford, 2009.
Edwards D. & Pilgram R., *The Romance of Metro-land*, Bloomsbury Books, London, 1986.
Gilliam T., *Twelve Monkeys*, UK/USA, 1995.
Grahame K., *The Wind in the Willows*, London, 1908.
Greene R., *The Adventures of Robin Hood*, Sapphire Films Ltd for ITC, UK, 1955–59.
Holt S., *Taste of Fear*, Hammer/Columbia, UK, 1961.
Horne M. A. C., *The Metropolitan Line*, Capital Transport, Harrow Weald, 2003.
Jerome J. K., *Three Men in a Boat*, London, 1889.
Journey Into Space, Charles Chilton, BBC, UK, 1953–2008.
Kemp W. A. G., *The Story of Northwood and Northwood Hills Middlesex*, Kemp, Northwood, 1955.
M@, *A Brief History of the Metropolitan Line*, https://londonist.com/london/history/a-brief-history-of-the-metropolitan-line, 03/12/24.
Lean D., *Brief Encounter*, UK, 1945.
Mankiewicz J. L. & Mamoulian R., *Cleopatra*, USA, 1963.
Mortimer J., *Paradise Postponed*, d. A. Rakoff, ITV, UK, 1986.
Portillo M., *Great British Railway Journeys*, BBC, UK, 2010–present.
Robertson D., *Tales of Wells Fargo*, Revue Productions TV, USA, 1957–62.
Starkey D., *Elizabeth: Apprenticeship*, Vintage, London, 2001.
Stokes T., *British Empire Exhibition: the forgotten event that took the world to Wembley*, https://www.bbc.com/uk-england-london-68733213, 06/02/25.
Turner H., *Secrets of Grim's Dyke: Playwrights,Romans,Spies?*, https://harrowonline.org/2016/04/06/the-secrets-of-grims-dyke:playwrights-romans-spies/#google-vignette, 05/02/06.
Vinterberg T., director, *Far From the Madding Crowd*, UK, 2013.
Waugh E., *Decline and Fall*, UK, 1928.
Wilson A. N., *After the Victorians*, Hutchinson, London, 2005.
Wolmar C., *The Subterranean Railway*, Atlantic Books, London, 2004.

INDEX

Places and stations are indexed under the name of the place, e.g Pinner refers to Pinner (place) and Pinner Station

Abbot of Bec 38
accidents 43–4, 124
Ace Cinema, Rayners Lane 90–1
Adam, Robert 20, 109
Ælfigu, Lady 105
Aldersgate Street (later Barbican) 45, 47
Aldgate 41, 74
Alexander, Bruce 95
Alexander de Isenhampstead 101
All Saints' Parish Church, Aylesbury 42
Amersham 6, 8, 42, 74, 92, 108–9, 117, 136
Amersham Cricket Club 109
Amersham Society 108, 109
Amersham-on-the-Hill 107
Amiconi, Giacomo 20
Armistice Day 28
Astley, Bernard 121
Astor, Mary and William 116
Athens-Piraeus Electric Railway 58
Ayers, Reverend C.F. 35
Aylesbury 37, 42, 105, 120, 123–4, 132, 134
    accident at 124
Aylesbury and Buckingham Railway (ABR) 41
Aylesbury Vale 42, 120, 123, 127
Aylesbury Vale Parkway 42, 134
Ayshford, Derek 102, 103

Baker Street Station 44–5, 46, 50, 58, 74, 136
Bakerloo Line 59, 88
Baldwin, Stanley 78
Barry, Charles 116
Batchworth Heath 17–19
    battle with visiting Londoners 19
Batchworth Lane 15, 20
Beacon Hill 120
Bec Helloin Abbey, Normandy 38
Bedford Arms, Chenies 103
Bedford Chapel, Chenies 103
Beeching, Dr Richard 1, 3, 6, 37, 40, 42, 133, 136
Belgian railways 2
Bell, John 132
Benedictine order 82
Berlin Airlift (1948) 34

Betjeman, John *see Metroland* (tv programme)
Bilyeau, Nancy 112–3
Birch, John 121
Bismarck (German U-boat) 34
Blankers-Koen, Fanny 69
Blomfield, Reginald 121
Bluebird Café, Northwood 29
Bo-Bo electric locomotives 41
Bob Hope Golf Classic 21
Bolbec, Hugh de 106
Bolebec, Isabel de 112–3
Boots booklovers' library 13
Borley, H.V. 122
Bourne Lane 90
Bridgeman, Charles 115
Brief Encounter (film) 29
Brill branch 127, 132–3
Bristol, Ernest and Freda 29–30
British empire 11, 65–6
British Empire Exhibition (1924-5) 64–9, 137
    'races in residence' displays 67
Bromige, Frank 90
Brook Street, Aylesbury 124
Brook Street Bureau (employment agency) 124
Brotherhood of St Francis of Wycombe 113
Brunel, Isambard Kingdom 6, 58
Bryson, Bill 131
Buckfast Abbey 82–3
Buckingham, 2nd Duke 114–5
Buckinghamshire County Museum 99, 127, 133
Buckinghamshire Railway Museum 134
Burn, William 115–6

Cadbury Chocolate Company 63
Cadsden, Bucks 119
Campion, Gerald 36
Capability Brown 126
Captain Bayley's Pleasure Grounds 91–2
Carreras, Sir James 25
Carter, Jimmy 116
Cassiobury Park, Watford 85
Catherine of Aragon 19

143

Catholic Schools 78
Catuvellauni tribe 80
Cavendish family 104, 106
Caxton, William 86
Cecil Park, Pinner 63
Cedars Estate, Rickmansworth 63, 98–9
Chalfont and Latimer 74, 100, 107
Chandos, Richard Temple-Nugent, Marquis 41–2
Channel Tunnel 34, 38, 56–7, 101
Charles I, King 75
Charles II, King 20, 115
Chatsworth House 104
Chaucer, Geoffrey 86
Chenies : A Brief History of the Village 101
Chenies Village 101–5
Chequers 120–1
Chesham 74, 81, 100, 105–7, 117
Chesham Bois 105–7
Chess Valley 100–1
Chesterton, G.K. 35
Cheyney, Alexander 101
Cheyney, Sir John 101
Cheyne, Thomas 101
Chiltern Hills 10–12, 99, 119–23, 138
    visionary experiences in 119–20
Chiltern Line 11–12, 37, 42, 74, 75, 124, 134, 135–6
Chorleywood 59, 86, 98
Christian, Princess of Schleswig-Holstein 32
Christie, Agatha 65
Church of England 31
church schools 78, 83
Churchill, Winston 78
Cipriani, Giovanni 20
Circle Line 41, 45, 74
Cistercian order 112–3
Clarke, C.W. 39
Claydon House, Aylesbury 42
Cleopatra (film) 67
Cliveden House 114–6
    fire 115
coal 46–7
Cockerell, Charles Robert 76
Collins, Wilkie 61
Comben and Wakeling (building company) 92
Compleat Angler Hotel, Marlow 111
Conrad, Joseph *Heart of Darkness* 111
Conservative Party 24, 34
Cook, Ernest 125
Coombe Hill 120, 123
    wildlife in 123
Corbett, Ronnie 21
Cornwall, G. 18
Council for the Protection of Rural England 109
crime 22, 27–8, 73, 122
Croke, Sir Robert 120
Cromwell, Thomas 20
Cromwell family 121
Croxley 84
Cunobelinus, King 120

Cushing, Peter 25
cycling 24
Cymbeline's Castle, Ellesborough 120

Danesfield House Hotel, Marlow 111
Dashwood, Sir Francis 113–4
De Vere Hotel, Latimer 104
Denison, Michael 109
Destaillleur, Gabriel-Hyppolyte 128
Deutsch, Oscar 91
Deutsche Bahn 12
Devonshire, Dukes of 106
Dickens, Charles 44–5, 61
Dilletanti Society 113
Dissolution of the Monasteries 20, 76, 82, 113
District Railway 89
Dodds Paper Mill 103
Dollis Hill 74
Dominican order 112
Downside Abbey 82–3
Drake, William 109
Draves, Victoria 70
Driscoll, James 44
Duchess of Connaught Red Cross Hospital 116
Duffield family 113, 114
Dunster station 14
Dutch railways 2

East India Company 20–1
Eastbury Avenue, Northwood 17
Eastbury Road 26
Eastcote 53, 88–9, 91–2
Ebury, Robert Grosvenor, Baron Ebury 19
Ebury family 21
Edgware Road 45, 49, 76
Edith, widow of Edward the Confessor 105–6
education 27
Edward I, King 101
Edward II, King 101
Edward VI, King 102
Edward VII, King 129
Edwards, Dennis 16, 39, 42–3, 45–7, 56, 96–7, 98, 132, 133
Elizabeth I, Queen 75
Ellesborough 119–20
Ellis, Ruth 108
Elm Park Court, Pinner 84
Elvstrom, Paul 70
Empire Day 28
Engel, Matthew 1–2
    Eleven Minutes Late: a Train Journey to the Soul of Britain 101
English Heritage (organisation) 122
Ernest Cook Trust 124
Ervine, St John 35
Euston Road accident 44
Exclusive Films Company 25

Far from the Madding Crowd (film) 42
Farr, Derek 24
Farringdon Station 4–5, 46, 61
Financial News 81

Index

Finchley Road 50, 58, 59, 74
Fleming, Peter 29
Fletcher, Madeleine 107
Fontainebleau Abbey 38
Ford, Gerald 21
Fowler, John 44, 45-6
France, fear of invasion by 57
Franklin, Benjamin 113
Frederick, Prince of Wales 113, 115
Fredriksson, Gert 70
French (clothing store) 13
French railways 32, 100

Ganz electrical system 49
Garner, James 21
gas lamps 47-8
Genevieve (film) 17
George V, King 65
German railways 2
Gilbert, William Schwenk 80
Gladstone, William 44, 58
Godwinson, Harold and Leofwine 105
Golders Green 64
Good Life, The (tv programme) 95
Goodall, Frederick 79
Gower Street 44, 46
Grahame, Kenneth *Wind in the Willows* 111-2
Grand Trunk Railway, Canada 58
Grange, The, Northwood 37-8
Grange Estate, Pinner 63
Gray, Dulcie 109
Great British Railway Journeys (tv programme) 131
Great Central Railway (GCR) 11, 36-7, 40, 42, 52, 56, 117, 132-5
Great Exhibition (1851) 66
Great Northern Railway 45
Great Southern Hotel, Éire 30
Great Western Railway 43, 45, 71, 132
Gregory, Edward 44
Gregson, John 17
Grey, Lady Mary 121
Grim's Dyke, Harrow 79-80
Gristwood, Mr 19
Grosvenor, Norman de L'Aigle 21
Grosvenor Cinema (later Ace; Odeon), Rayners Lane 90
Grosvenor Cinema/Bar Experience 91
Grosvenor family 20, 21
Grove Hill, Harrow 75
Guide to the Extension Line 62

Halton POW camp 122-3
Hamilton, George, Earl of Orkney 115
Hammer Films 25
Hammersmith 45, 54
Hampden family 125
Hancock, Tony 37
Harding, Thomas 106
Harrow 37, 51, 74-6, 79, 117, 132, 136
Harrow Garden Village 63, 90

Harrow Road 76
Harrow School 41, 75-8
  fagging system 76-7
Harrow-on-the-Hill 50, 55, 65, 74, 88-9, 135-6
Harrowonline (website) 81-2
Hartwell House 124-6
Hartwell Observatory 125
Hatch End 83
Hawtrey, William 121
Hearn, A.J. 47-8
Helen Hoare Collection, Ruislip 96-7
Hellfire Club 113-4
Henry I, King 112
Henry VII, King 102 113, 121
Henry VIII, King 19-20, 76, 102
High and Over (architectural style) 92
High Wycombe 132
Hillingdon 54, 58
Historic England (organisation) 122
Historic Hotel Group 125
Hodgkison, Alfred 19
Holkham Hall, Norfolk 109
Holy Trinity Church, Northwood 31
Home Farm, Rickmansworth 18
Home Rule for Ireland Bill 58
Hornby model railways 13-14
Horne, Mike 41-2, 49, 51, 52, 63-5, 88-9, 135
horror films 25
Howard, Catherine 19
Howard, Trevor 29
HS1 railway 101
HS2 railway 10, 37, 40, 108-9, 123-4, 133, 138
Hugh Sexey Church Middle School 15

Ickenham 53, 88, 92
Icknield Way 120
immigration 28, 57
Inner Circle 46, 50-1, 52, 55
Intercolonial Railway, Canada 58
Isen, Bavaria 101-2

Jacobs, David 91
James, M.R. 119-20
Jerome, Jerome K. *Three Men in a Boat* 111-2
Joel Street bridge, Northwood Hills 38
John I, King 112
John Lewis (department store) 63
Johnson, Celia 29
Johnston, Mindy 69
Journey Into Space (radio programme) 91
Jubilee Line 41, 59

Keeler, Christine 116
Keene, Henry 126
Keith, Penelope 95
Kemp, W.A.G. 17-19, 21, 26, 28, 32, 35, 37-9
Kendall, Kay 17

145

Kewferry Road, Northwood 95
Kilburn 52, 58, 59, 74
King Charles' Well 75
King's College, Cambridge 38
King's Cross Station 43–5
Kingsbury 59
Kingsbury Garden Village 63
Kingswood branch 133
Kirby, Annie 132

Labour Party 1, 27, 34, 83
Lake Como Railway 49
Lambert, Constant 70
Latimer House 104
    IRA bombing of 105
Lawrence, D.H. 22
Leadbetter, Stiff 109
Lee, Arthur, 1st Viscount Lee 120–1
Lee, Dr John 125
Lee, Sammy 70
Lee, Sir Charles 125
Leoni, Giacomo 115
Leventon, Annabel 100
Leventon family 100
Lever, William, Viscount Leverhulme 21
Liberty William 105
Liberty Tomb, Chess Valley 105
Liberty's (department store) 105
Lodge Hill 127
Lollards 106
London and Birmingham Railway 83
London College of Divinity 38
London Transport Passenger Board 62
Longhurst, Henry 30
Louis Stanislas Xavier, Count of Provence (later Louis XVIII) 125
Lowndes family 106
Lyon, John 41, 75–6

M25 ring road 59, 85, 88
Mad Bess Wood 19
Manor of the More 16, 19, 26
Marie Josephine, wife of Louis XVIII 125
Marlborough Road 59
Marlow, Buckinghamshire 111
Marylebone Station 12, 37, 74, 133, 135
Masefield, John 35
Master Cutler (steam train) 36
Mathias, Bob 70
Mazawattee tea 98
McArthur, Sir William, Lord Mayor of London 43
Medmenham Abbey 112–3
Merchant Taylors' School 19, 26, 30–1, 78
Metro-land 5–10, 62–73
    advertising for 71
    architectural styles in 92
    gender roles in 60, 71
    housing in 63, 71–2
    post WWII era 59–60, 72, 95, 138
    promotion of 63–4
    property prices in 92–3, 98–9

Metroland (tv programme) 59–60, 67, 75, 81, 85, 98, 107
Metropolitan Line 4, 7, 10, 40–8
    abandoned stations 3
    electrification of 49–54
    grand opening day 44–5
    overground stations 58, 74, 137
    Saturday Pullman trains 100
    signalling systems for 135–6
    see also specific places and stations
Metropolitan Railway County Estates Ltd 62–3
Middlesex 14–15
Middlesex Regiment 15
Midsomer Murders (tv programme) 119
Mill End 86
Milne, A.A. and 'Hundred Acre Wood' 10, 22, 131–2
Modernism in Metroland 92, 136
Monmouth, Scott James, 1st Duke 20
Moonies (Unification Church) 78
Moor Park 15–17, 20, 53, 122, 136
    property prices in 161–7
Moor Park Arts Society *Moor Park Mansion* 20
Moor Park Farm 19, 26
Moor Park Golf Club 17, 19–22
Moorgate Station 45
More, Kenneth 17
More, Thomas and Robert 113
Mortimer, John 112
Mount Vernon Hospital 32–3
Mountbatten, Edwina 78

Nash, Dr 38
National Defence College 104
National Trust 114–5, 122, 123, 125, 128–30
Neasden depot 49–50, 58, 59, 63
Nehru, Jawarhalal 78
Newgate, last public hanging at (1868) 61
Nightingale, Florence 42
North Harrow 37, 53, 84
North Metropolitan Railway Act (1854) 43
Northwick Park 54, 74
Northwood 13–15, 29, 33–9, 47, 53, 81, 94
    local shops in 94
Northwood Boys' Club (later St John's Boys' Club) 27
Northwood College 35
Northwood Hills 38–9, 53
Northwood Literary Society 35
Northwood Preparatory School Trust (Terry's) Ltd 26
Norton, Daniel 18
Nottingham 133

O2 Arena 72
Odeon Cinema, Rayners Lane 90–1
Odo, Bishop of Bayeux 106
Offa, King of Mercia 18, 26, 85
Ogbourne Priory, Willtshire 38
Olympic Games (1948) 64–5, 69–70
    women contestants 69–70

Index

Orwell, George 27, 73
Ostiarius, Elias 121
Oxford-Cambridge link 134

Paddington Station 43–5
Palmerston, Henry, Viscount Palmerston 78
Papp, László 70
Paradise Postponed (tv programme) 112
Pavlow, Muriel 24
PC49 (radio programme) 25
Peachey (builder) 39
Pearson, Charles *A Brief History of the Metropolitan Line* 42–3, 45
Peel, Robert 78
Peninsular War 15
Peverel, William 125
Piccadilly Line 88
Pilgram, Ronald 16, 39, 42–3, 45–7, 56, 96–7, 98, 132, 133
Pinewood Studios 67
Pinner 37, 47, 51, 53, 81–4
Pinner Fair 84
Pinner Lane 90
Pinner Wood Estate 84
Pollitt, William 132
Poplars, The, Ruislip 97
Portillo, Michael 131
Portland Road (later Great Portland Street) 44–5, 46
Powell, Enoch 57
Preston Road 74
Princes Risborough 120, 132
Profumo, John 116
public schools 77–8
Putin, Vladimir 34

Quainton Hill 41
Quainton Road 42, 133–4
Queensberry, Marquess of 113

RAF Coastal Command 29, 33–4
railway carriages
 1st class 51–2
 2nd class 51
 Dreadnought design 52
 interior furnishings in 51
 ladies only 51
Railway Magazine 122–3
railway trains
 diesel trains 5, 14
 electric locomotives 5, 14, 41, 50–2
 newspaper trains 124
 steam trains 4–5, 36–7, 46–7, 107
Railway Traveller's Handy Book of Hints, Suggestions and Advice (1862) 2
railways
 advertisements for 4
 cuts in services 1–3
 heritage railway volunteers 3, 14, 37, 130, 134
 see also specific railway companies
Rank Organisation 91

Rayners Lane 53, 79, 84, 89–90
Red Lion pub, Wendover 123
religion 31, 27–8
Repton, Humphrey 109
Rhodes, Henry 121
Richmond 54
Rickmansworth 37, 47, 81, 84–6, 117
Rickmansworth Historical Society 98
River Brent 59
River Chess 85–6, 100, 103, 105
River Colne 85–6
River Misbourne 109
River Thames 85, 111–2
Robertson, Dale 4
Robinson, A. (builder) 89
Rothschild, Baron Ferdinand de 127–8
Rothschild, James de 128–9
Rothschild family 127–9
Rous, Thomas Bates 20–1
Rowntree Chocolate Company 63
Royal Bank of Scotland 21
Royal Meteorological Society 125
Royal Swedish Railway Company 2
Ruislip 37, 50, 89, 95–7
Ruislip Lido 95–6
Ruislip Manor 53
Russell, Dukes of Bedford 103
Russell, John 102–3, 121
Russell, Reverend Lord Wriothesley 102
Ryder, Richard 19

Sadleir, John 2–3
St George, John 38
St Helen's School, Northwood 35
St John the Baptist Church, Pinner 82
St John's Wood 58, 59
St Lawrence Drive, Eastcote 92
St Martin's Preparatory School, Northwood 22–4
St Mary's, Harrow 74, 82
St Mary's, Rickmansworth 86
St Michaels Parish Church, Chenies 103
Saint Peter and Paul, Ellesborough 120
St Vincent's Nursing Home 33
St Vincent's Orthopaedic Hospital 33
Sandwich, John Montagu, Earl of Sandwich 113, 114
Sandy Lodge Golf Club 17
Sandy Lodge 16, 21, 53
Sangster, Jimmy 25
Selbie, Robert 62
Seymour family 106
Shakespeare Cliff, Devon 57
Shardeloes, Amersham 109
Shasore, Neal 66–7
Shaw, Richard Norman 79
Siddons, Sarah 41
Sisters of Charity of St Vincent de Paul 133
Smyth, William Henry 125
Soane, Sir John 126
South Yorkshireman (steam train) 36
South-Eastern Railway

147

Tracks: A Journey Through Metro-Land

Spanish flu pandemic 28, 66, 91
Speedwriting (shorthand system) 124
Stanmore branch 41, 59
Starkey, David *Elizabeth : Apprenticeship* 121
Starmer, Keir 10, 14
Stokes, Tim 65–6
street traders 99
Styles, Benjamin Haskins 20
Surplus Lands Committee 62
Sutherland, Duchess 116
Swedish railways 2–3
Swiss Cottage 58, 59

Tales of Wells Fargo (tv programme) 4
Taste of Fear (film) 25
television sets 94–5
Terry, Francis John 26–7
Terry's Preparatory School, Northwood 26
Thatcher, Margaret 120
Thornhill, Sir James 20
Three Rivers Council 21, 85
Throssell, Eric 126
Touch of Frost, A (tv programme) 95
trains *see* electric locomotives; newspaper trains; railway carriages; steam trains
Turner, Harry 79, 80
Turpin, Dick 18
Tussaud family 30
Twelve Monkeys (film) 18
Tyrwhitt-Drake family 109

United States railways 2
Uxbridge 74, 79, 135
Uxbridge branch 50, 53, 88–93

ventilation shafts 47
Vere, Robert de 112–3
Verney, Sir Harry 41–2
Verney Junction 8–9, 41, 107, 134
Victoria, Queen 57, 116, 128, 129
Voysey, Charles 98

Waddesdon Manor 127–9
walking 118
Warrender, George 115
Watford 64, 74, 84–6, 135
Watkin, Dom Aelred 55

Watkin, Sir Edward 5, 8, 34, 40, 49, 54, 55–61, 68, 136–7
Watson, Richard 109
Waugh, Evelyn *Decline and Fall* 139
Weedon, George 97
Welby, Justin, former Archbishop of Canterbury 28
Wells, H.G. 131–2
Wembley Park 51, 59, 63, 64–5, 67–8
Wembley Stadium 69–70
Wembley Tower 34, 49, 56, 68
Wendover 123
West Hampstead 58, 59
West Harrow 53, 88
West Hyde 86
West Ruislip 88
West Somerset Line 14
West Wycombe 113
Westinghouse Electrical Manufacturing Company 49–50, 51–2
Wilkinson, W.H. 44
Willesden 52
William, Duke of Normandy, the Conqueror 38–9, 106
Williams, John 42–3
Williams, Robert 21
Williams Deacon Bank 21
Wilson, A.N. *After the Victorians* 71
Winde, William 115
Woburn Abbey 112
  Animal Kingdom 68
Wolf Hall (tv programme) 19–20
Wolmar, Christian 71
Wolsey, Cardinal Thomas 16, 19–20, 26, 86
Woodroffe, Lionel W. 22–4
Wotton Station 132–3
Wotton Tramway 127
WWI: 7, 26, 62, 66, 89–90, 91, 116
WWII: 33–4, 92, 104

Ye Olde Greene Manne pub, Rickmansworth 18–19
Yvonne Arnaud Theatre, Guildford 95

Zátopek, Emil 69–70
Zoroastrian Centre 90–1